AF398942

THE AUTONOMY OF THEORY

TICINO ARCHITECTURE AND ITS CRITICAL RECEPTION

IRINA DAVIDOVICI

INTRODUCTION

Only a minority of the buildings erected in any one place at one time are designed by architects. A yet smaller part of this minority is caught in the crosshairs of critical attention. The very few buildings that reach beyond a small, local audience of users thus become part of the architecture discourse. Their actual spatial and material presence is doubled by another parallel existence: as images printed on paper, bound within the covers of architectural publications. Moreover, the architects with the most avid following are almost never those who build the most, but those whose output—whether built, spoken, or written—is best suited to the communications channels of critical discourse.

This double condition is reflected in Adrian Forty's deft transposition of Roland Barthes's *The Fashion System* (1967) to architecture, which allows it to be understood as a system of buildings, images, and words.[1] According to this tripartite structure, "architecture" is a complex cultural construct that comprises, beyond the built artifacts, their representations through drawings and photographs, as well as the textual commentaries provided by architects, critics, and historians. The built, which we associate with architecture proper, is usually fixed and only available to a limited audience of users and visitors. Its dissemination therefore depends on its circulation through images and words, historically on paper. Without printed (or digital) text, drawings, and photographs, there is no architectural discourse.

This book is less about buildings than about the words and images that enable the formation of discourse. It focuses on the widespread coverage of the architecture projects built in the Italian-speaking Swiss region of Ticino in the 1960s, 1970s, and 1980s. Although only a small part of the overall development in this relatively remote part of Europe, this recent Ticinese architecture caused a profusion of publications of varying quality and scope. This written production had the

---

1 Adrian Forty, *Words and Buildings: A Vocabulary of Modern Architecture* (London: Thames & Hudson, 2000), 13.

peculiar consequence of attracting architects and students from afar, enticing them to see the buildings on site. Alone or in groups, organized or informally, architects descended upon public and private properties alike, knocking on doors, scaling fences, peering in between shutters. Coupled with the irritated tolerance of locals, a species of professional tourism flourished, reinforced by the architecture leaflets distributed in regional tourist offices. Together with study-trip readers and architecture guides, these leaflets were the fringe outputs of a more substantial stream of architectural publications, which ranged from coffee-table monographs to architecture anthologies and specialized reference books. To attain this level of attention, Ticino's modern buildings were allotted an additional function to those for which they had been built: as manifestations of an architectural discourse. As part of this further agenda, they were covered, disseminated, and commented upon through the portable medium of the printed page.

Why did this happen in Ticino? At once transitional and insular, edged up against the natural barrier of the Alps, Switzerland's Italian-speaking canton has for centuries channeled the cultural and economic traffic between a nominal north and south of Europe.[2] In the early twentieth century, it became a destination for artists from regions further north, whose inputs helped conflate *Neue Sachlichkeit* and the Italian *razionalismo*. Between the two world wars, these influences blended in a handful of villas and public buildings, including the Bauhaus-style hotel Monte Verità by German architect Emil Fahrenkamp (1927) and the Cantonal Library of Lugano (1940) by Rino Tami. But in themselves, these facts fail to explain why a remote region of less than 3,000 square kilometers, in its totality less populous than the single

2 In the fifteenth century, the region passed from the control of Italian city-republics to that of Swiss cantons north of the Alps. The canton of Ticino was founded in 1803 as one of nineteen cantons of the new Swiss Confederation, resulting from the unification of the Helvetic Republic cantons of Bellinzona and Lugano. See Raffaello Ceschi, *Geschichte des Kantons Tessin* (Frauenfeld: Huber, 2003), 35–55.

city of Zurich, would become an international center of architecture during the 1970s and 1980s. The underlying reason was the canton's cultural orientation towards Italy. Through Ticino, topical design methods and ideologies imported from Italian architecture were transferred across the Alps. At the same time, if earlier generations of Ticinese architects had been trained in Italy, during and after the Second World War their educational center moved to ETH Zurich. This not only created a new bridge with the German-speaking discourse but also a professional network developed during decades of collective and individual practice.

These intra-architectural factors are still not enough to explain Ticinese architecture's success. This was above all a matter of fortunate timing. During the decisive decades of postwar growth, the canton was transformed into a center of light industry—much to the detriment of its natural landscape and historical heritage. This economic boom went hand in hand with increases in population and prosperity, social mobility, and the modernization of ways of life, from living standards to education reform. Thus the architectural production that came to be was aligned with the values and aspirations of its commissioners, in the form of an educated professional middle class. In short: the success of this so-called autonomous architecture was, in fact, dependent upon the social, political, and economic conditions of its production.

Despite the common circumstances of the protagonists—their professional formation, initial exposure, related design approaches—the critical attention on Ticino architects was and remains unequally distributed. Some became household names with international currency (Mario Botta, Aurelio Galfetti, Luigi Snozzi, Livio Vacchini), while others (Peppo Brivio, Mario Campi, Tita Carloni, Giancarlo Durisch, Bruno Reichlin, Fabio Reinhart, Flora Ruchat-Roncati) gained professional and institutional recognition mostly within Switzerland. Despite this uneven spread of cultural capital, the intellectual legacy of this generation of Ticinese architects is still perceived as primarily collective. Through the combined means of professional coverage, teaching positions, exhibitions, and monographs, it influenced subsequent generations of architects in and beyond Switzerland. In many ways, their assembled production contributed to the crystallization, if not generalization, of a design method that still continues to dominate sections of the architecture scene today.

The Ticino episode is uniquely positioned to allow a more general investigation of the ways in which the critical reception of buildings intervenes in the production of architecture. From this perspective, Ticinese architecture is a point of entry to understanding the role of the architectural discourse generated by implacable, often opaque, mechanisms of critical evaluation. This extended essay traces the instrumentality of these critical views, not only in shaping the public perception of the built production but in conferring professional credibility upon their authors, sometimes even with political consequences. The relatively controlled field of this Ticino architecture thus allows the reconstruction of a dialogue between architectural discourse and its wider socio-cultural sphere.

The chapters that follow provide an alternative history of late modern Ticinese architecture, shifting the attention from the built production to the discourse that accompanied it. "The Paper Apparatus" dissects the anatomy of the catalogue to the 1975 exhibition *Tendenzen: Neuere Architektur im Tessin*. Drawing parallels between the exhibition catalogue's graphic layout and its theoretical framework, it argues that the production of the catalogue was the first step in a process of assimilation of buildings into text. The next chapter overviews the built architecture as a theoretical catalyst, which was later conveniently packaged into the compact narrative of the *Tendenzen* exhibition. "The Currency of Tendency" then focuses on the exhibition and its immediate reception, showing how the international currency of the built production grew at the expense of a finer-grained understanding of the forces that had shaped its existence. This is followed by the examination of the curated theoretical arguments in "The Emancipation of Theory" that inscribed the work—buildings and architects' texts—into the discourse on architectural autonomy.

With increased theoretical currency came a parallel external projection by another architectural critic upon the Ticinese work. The next chapter, "Critical Constructs and the Myth of the Ticino," argues that Kenneth Frampton's inclusion of Ticinese architecture in his reading of critical regionalism constituted an act of "operative criticism."[3] Not only did Frampton put into circulation the construct of a (at the time non-existent) "School of the Ticino," but by singling out Mario Botta as one of the architect-auteurs of critical regionalism, he inadvertently disturbed a delicate professional ecology, giving rise to a new sense of hierarchy and competition.

The brief intermezzo, "The Alps as Cultural Boundary," explores the historical imprint of the Alps as the linguistic and cultural border between Ticino and the rest of Switzerland. It shows how the region's geo-cultural closeness to Italy and remoteness from the Swiss highlands colored the intellectual relations between the Italian-Swiss, German-Swiss, and Italian protagonists of the 1970s architectural exchanges. The interlude also serves to highlight the caesura between the highbrow readings of external critics such as Steinmann and Frampton and the more popular, less processed readings of Ticino architecture they invited. It is followed by the chapter "Literatures of a Third Kind," which focuses on the gray literature, readers, travel guides, and monographic anthologies that followed in the footsteps of

---

3 Coined by Manfredo Tafuri, the term "operative criticism" denotes the practice of instrumentalizing or manipulating historical interpretation to suit contemporary agendas: Manfredo Tafuri, *Teorie e storia dell'architettura* (Rome: Laterza, 1968). While Tafuri used it in a derogatory way, the situatedness of any historian in a given historical context suggests that such contaminations are to some extent inevitable.

the initial theoretical readings, with decidedly mixed results. This creates some contrast to the texts described in the following chapter, "The Resistance of the Local," in which local witnesses and involved actors pushed back against the profusion of unhelpful myths in the multiple external readings of Ticinese architecture. While not as widely disseminated on account of their regional focus—not to mention the lack of translations—these local commentaries, both intra- and trans-disciplinary, possess the acuity and complexity lacking in other somewhat schematic theoretical readings of Ticinese architecture. "Between Autonomy and Realism" closes the cycle of theoretical interpretations with insights into a new built production, indicating the implications that the Ticino discourse had for architecture in Switzerland and beyond. It argues that the theory extracted from the buildings aided the crystallization of a design method placed at the intersection of "autonomous" and "realist" readings of architecture. The final chapter, "Communities of Practice as Regional *Tendenze*," looks at a longer-term legacy that *Tendenzen* has had in the emergence of new regional *tendenze*—and corresponding professional networks—taking as examples Britain and Belgium.

In sum, this extended essay is not another historical monograph on the architecture of the Ticino from the 1960s and 1970s. Rather, it extends the meaning of "historiography" to examine not only the written histories but also the architectural monographs, anthologies, journals, newspapers, and catalogue exhibitions that launched the Ticinese architecture of this period into the international discourse. It argues that the processes of critical reception, ranging from highbrow to popular, from academic to journalistic, from profoundly insightful to trite, have concrete effects on the very architecture that brought them into existence. These effects are not only cultural but also material and political, and they resonate beyond the development of individual careers. At the core of the argument is therefore the agency of theory writing as it emancipates itself from the buildings on which it was based in the first place. Thus seen, this book is closer to the history of a historiography—tracing its impact on the built environment, on professional structures, and on the integrity of architectural discourse.

The autonomy of theory described in this book is not the same as the autonomy of the architecture, which populates a related, yet distinct theoretical *topos*. In the context of this study, which is focused on the critical reception of Ticinese projects, the distinction is to some extent blurred by their association with the tenets of architectural autonomy. And yet, although critical readings explicitly used architectural autonomy as a common denominator to group the heterogeneous production of 1960s and 1970s Ticino, the autonomy of theory proposed here is a parallel, distinct proposition: a precondition for the exchange and regeneration of architectural ideas. It is what allows professional circles belonging to different places and times to share a common agenda and develop and use a common set of design tools. The autonomy of theory ensures the adaptability of these tools and their wider circulation through the written architectural discourse. As dictated by this thread, we begin neither with built nor with projected architecture, but rather with their repackaging via a paper apparatus: the medium of the printed page.

THE PAPER APPARATUS

A blueprint-blue cover, white lettering, landscape format. Still in print decades after its original publication in 1975, the catalogue *Tendenzen: Neuere Architektur im Tessin* has acquired a cult following, despite its modest production values. Of all the exhibition catalogues produced by the ETH Zurich Department of Architecture in the 1970s, it is one of the most familiar and widely circulated, with three successive editions between 1975 and 1976 and a facsimile reprint in 2010.[4] The horizontal format of the series replicates Le Corbusier's eight-volume *Oeuvre complète*: a standard of the times, which allowed the optimal reproduction of working drawings and photographs.[5] By prioritizing architectural iconography over the written word, the ETH catalogues claimed their place among "real" architects' books, just as how the exhibitions program targeted students and practitioners rather than the general public. And yet, while other publications from the series explored architecture's wider social and historical dimensions, the *Tendenzen* catalogue focused on a contemporaneous, local architecture. An intra-disciplinary catalogue of buildings and projects, it was conceived as a tool for practitioners, a template for professional knowledge. It aimed to be a design method bound in paper.

4 These volumes reflected an ambitious and varied program of exhibitions at the Architecture Department of ETH Zurich, starting in 1968 with the monographic show *Angelo Mangiarotti* initiated by ETH professor Heinz Ronner, who curated the overall exhibitions series until 1975. From 1976 onwards, the exhibitions division (Organisationsstelle für Ausstellungen der Architekturabteilung, or OAA) became part of the Institute for the History and Theory of Architecture (Institut für Geschichte und Theorie der Architektur, or gta Institute), and later became known as gta Ausstellungen (gta Exhibitions). Between 1969 and 1979, ETH Zurich held shows on crucial contemporary figures such as Louis Kahn, James Stirling, Oswald Mathias Ungers, and Aldo Rossi; classical modernists Mart Stam, Erich Mendelsohn, and Johannes Duiker; Swiss architects such as Alberto Sartoris, Rudolf Olgiati, and Pierre Zoelly; Swiss construction systems and authorless architecture; as well as on Henri Labrouste and Inigo Jones.

5 Willy Boesiger, *Le Corbusier: Les dernières œuvres / The Last Works / Die letzten Werke*, vol. 8 (Zurich: Les Editions d'architecture Artemis, 1965). The eighth and last volume completed a series begun in 1929 by Swiss architect and editor Willy Boesiger, the box set of which was first reprinted in 1970.

This catalogue accompanied the 1975 exhibition *Tenden-zen: Neuere Architektur im Tessin*, which featured forty-eight projects from twenty-one practices from the Italian-speaking canton of Ticino (fig. 1). The selection of projects explic-itly prioritized buildings—private houses, educational and leisure complexes, restoration projects—that could be dis-cussed in terms of material and typological presence, in other words in autonomous, intra-disciplinary terms. This prefer-ence can also be read in the sparse design of the sixty-six black-and-white display panels, favoring the conventional modes of architectural representation: plans, sections, and photographs.

Both catalogue and exhibition made little attempt to situate the production, with barely a mention of the socio-economic, demographic, and cultural agendas that enabled these privileged sites of architectural experimentation. There was no explanation for the predominance of private one-family houses and historical restorations—programs hardly characteristic of postwar economic growth—or as to why so many nurseries, primary schools, and gymnasia had been built in a small territory in such a short time. There was no mention of the pedagogical reform that underlined these progressive designs, nor of the cantonal officials who had fought to commission young, unproven architects. Instead, the architectural context was reduced to the dramatic to-pography visible in photographs, picturesquely framing the buildings on display.

This decontextualizing curatorial approach is mirrored in the graphic design strategies that organize the catalogue's contents. The page layouts mirror the role of the exhibition as an abstractive interpretative device. Just as the landscape format was adopted to prioritize architectural representation (as shown above), here the strict separation of "text pages" from "visual information pages" suggests the application of a modernist zoning approach to the scale of the book. From the second edition onwards, a final section of dense text,

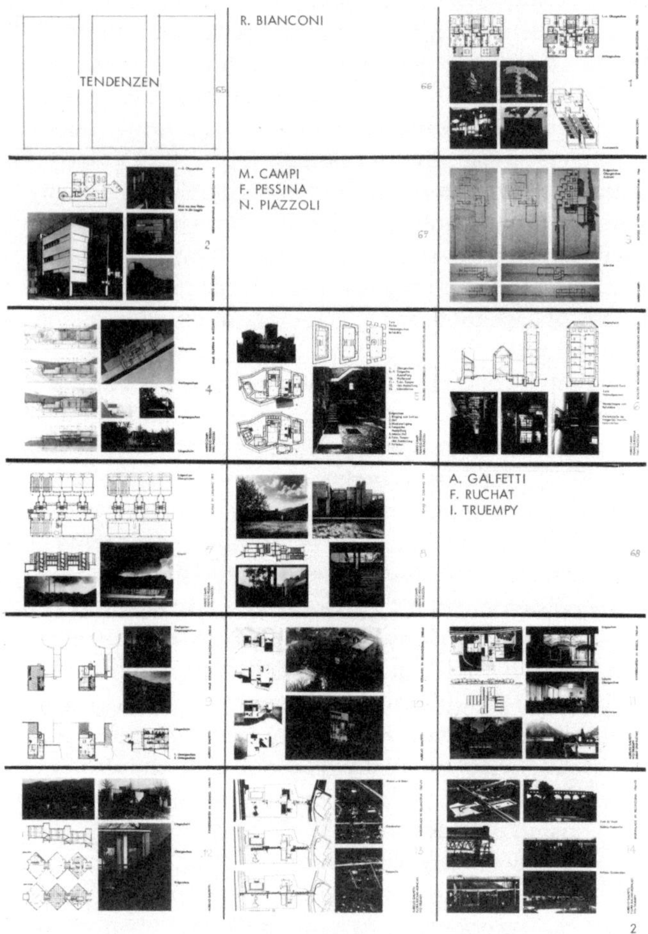

1   First of five A4 inventory sheets showing the *Tendenzen* exhibition panels in reduced size. The original A0 panels and A4 catalogue pages share the same layout.

printed on yellow paper, was added, containing the translations of all the texts, originally published in German, into English and Italian. The choice of languages in this additional section acknowledges, beyond the initial audience of German-Swiss architects, a wider international audience, as well as a regional Ticinese one. It simultaneously represents the return of the material to its sources and its projection, through the language of greater circulation, into a global Western discourse.

The pages dedicated to visual information are composed according to strict homogenizing principles. Photographs and drawings are all subjected to the same set of basic reprographic techniques, flattened to a common grainy black and white (fig. 2). About a third of the catalogue pages are small-scale reproductions of the full-size exhibition panels, which were mounted as A0-sized assemblies of photocopied drawings and photographs. Focusing on buildings as end products, the exhibition omitted original drawings and photographic prints, and so dispensed with situating the processes of design. No trace of tracing paper, no material collage, no ink line from the tip of a Rotring pen late at night disturbed the certainty of the project as built. By omitting the gray-scale hesitation of pencil lines, sticky tape and erasure marks, the exhibition replicated the common horizon of architectural criticism: detached from the original creative context of the design process and primarily dedicated to its analysis.

The preparatory drawings and maquettes of the catalogue reveal precisely the hidden moments of the (graphic) design process. Independently of its contents, which are discussed in a later chapter, the catalogue layout offers some clues as to the attitudes underlying the curator's reception of Ticinese architecture. Namely, a parallel can be constructed between the graphic principles governing the space of the pages and the curatorial strategies at work in the exhibition. Both illustrate a critical reinterpretative process, through

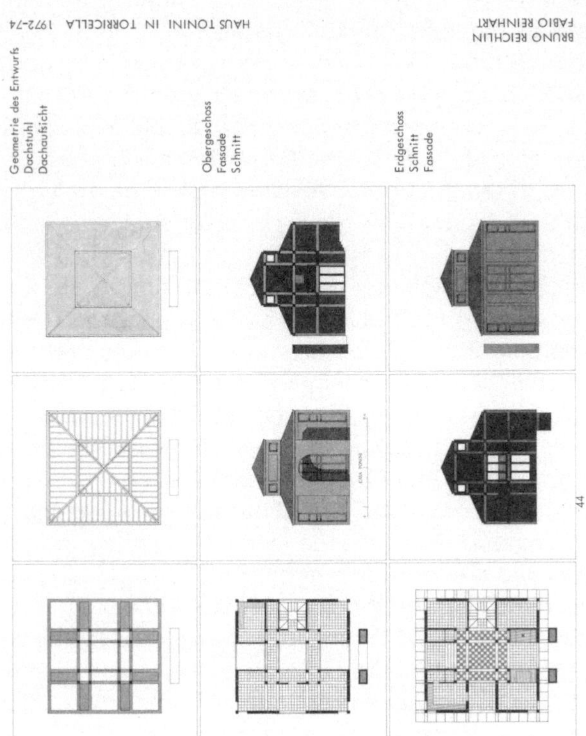

2 Exhibition panel of Bruno Reichlin and Fabio Reinhart's drawings for Casa Tonini in Torricella, 1972–74. Here shown in the *Tendenzen* catalogue, 1975, p. 44.

which an external matrix is imposed upon a heterogeneous set of materials, flattening the initial variety of their positions. As replicated by the production processes within the catalogue, the curatorial approach can be read as a homogenizing and simplifying device. But the drastic reduction of drawings amounts to an act of reprographic violence, through which the inner unity, scale, and materiality of the original materials is reduced to the common denominator of easily digestible signifiers.

In the *Oxford Dictionary of English*, "catalogue" is defined as a systematic and "complete list of items." As literary genre, the exhibition catalogue derives from the eighteenth-century *catalogue raisonné*, "a descriptive catalogue of works of art with explanations and scholarly comments."[6] The catalogue is essentially a rationalizing device, ordering a random assortment of items into a common matrix. In the case of the *Tendenzen* catalogue, the systemic nature of the layout production mirrors the curatorial strategies governing its content.

If catalogues commonly reproduce the works on display in an exhibition, in this case the same layouts were used at different scales for the A0 exhibition panels and A4 book pages. With our understanding conditioned by the reproduction of works of art in the printed medium, we could easily assume that the original panels were reduced eightfold and neatly collected to form the catalogue. However, the production materials reveal the opposite, whereby the common format was primarily conceived for the page, then blown up to panel size. This primacy of the catalogue helped systematize the heterogeneous visual material gathered for the exhibition, rather than the other way around. Following the curatorial selection, the graphic designer had to keep track of hundreds of drawings and photographs, representing the architectural projects at different scales, in different locations, through

6 "Catalogue," entry in Catherine Soanes and Angus Stevenson, eds., *Oxford Dictionary of English*, 2nd ed., rev. (Oxford: Oxford University Press, 2005), 271.

different techniques. Indeed, the residual material from the catalogue production attests to the invisible presence of a key homogenizing device, introduced as a graphic common denominator for this random material: the grid (fig. 3).

The *Tendenzen* catalogue maquettes show how gridded layouts determined the sheet margins, size, and position of text and pictures, providing the underlying principles for the distribution of images on the page. The grid allowed for different ways of dividing the space of each page into sections, to which individual images were assigned. This formatting process—today internalized in the opaque workings of computer software—is visible in the several drafts produced for each page. Each of the sixty-six page or panel layouts was subjected to at least three design stages. First, a set of small images, printed as thumbnails, were distributed across the grid, photocopied onto the paper. Then every image was placed, and its contours marked in red felt tip pen on the grid (fig. 4). The resulting assembly of photographs and drawings was individually tested and revised before being reproduced as a catalogue page (figs. 5, 6). The pages thus physically collated were photographed on lithographic film, and the A4 negatives projected at the scale of exhibition panels.

Through this sequential process, the material—whether photographs of models or completed buildings, small sketches or large drawings, drawn in pencil on tracing paper or atmospherically airbrushed—was brought to a state of visual equivalence. Fit into the concealed logic of the grid, the sum of these materials amounted to an artificial construct whose unity was implied in the space of the page. This process of editing and identification of a visual common denominator matched the curatorial treatment of the various projects, helping insert them into a common overarching narrative. As such, the catalogue's graphic production is akin to the architectural historian's—or curator's—attempt to construct a coherent reading of their material, at the expense of its inherent complexity. The exhibition sought

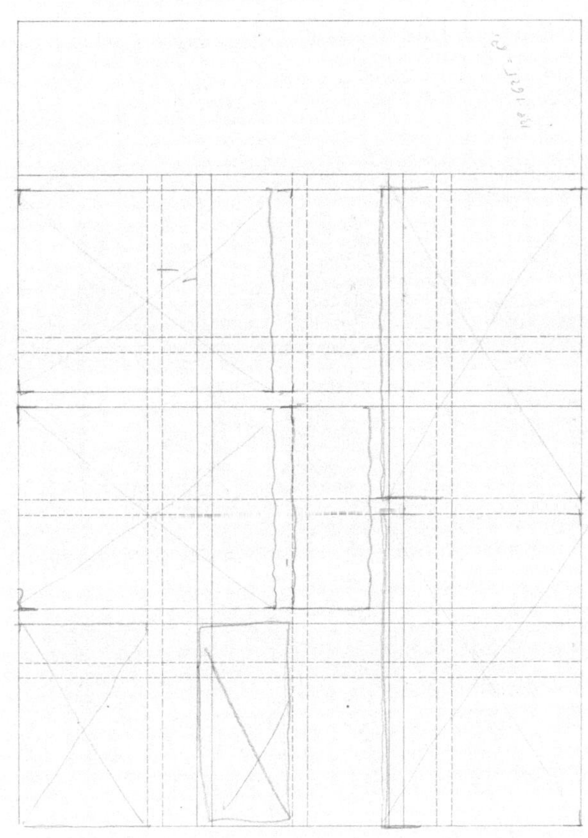

3　Each catalogue page or panel is organized by a gridded template that is only visible on maquette sheets (here shown in blue, with red corrections).

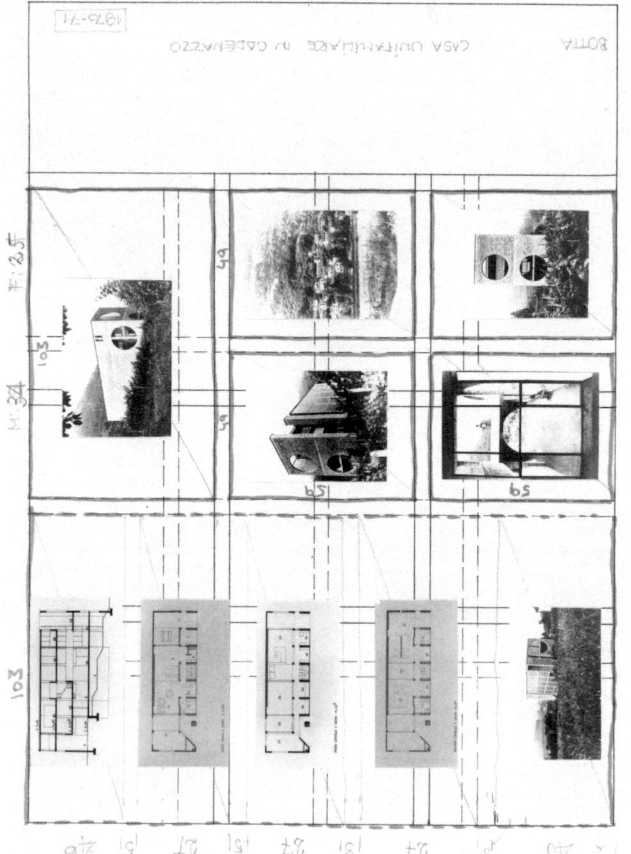

4   Mario Botta's House in Cadenazzo: image selection for layout

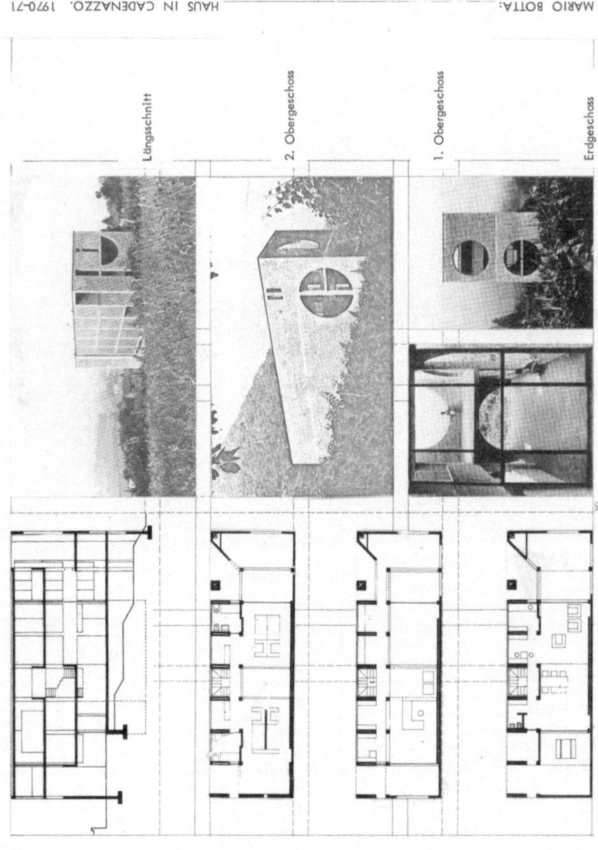

5   Mario Botta's House in Cadenazzo: image placement and adjustments

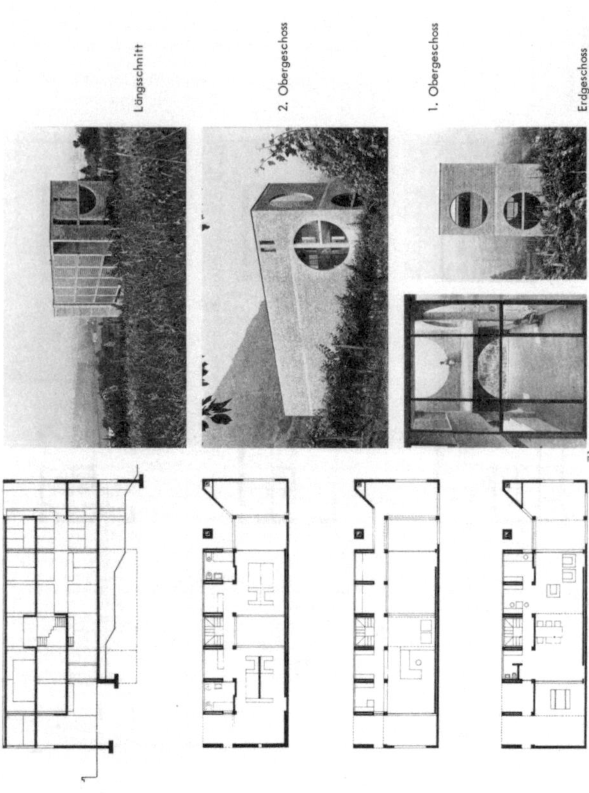

6   Mario Botta's House in Cadenazzo: finished page in the *Tendenzen* catalogue, 1975, p. 71

to counteract the inevitable heterogeneity of an assorted group of Ticinese professionals by constructing a common theoretical narrative for their projects.

In the process, the details and textures of the constructed building and architectural drawings were brushed aside. One illustrative example of the resulting loss is the visual material accompanying one of the most radical buildings featured in the original exhibition. Giancarlo Durisch's house and atelier in Riva San Vitale, barely finished at the time of the exhibition, can be seen as an almost literal manifestation of architectural autonomy. The two mirrored buildings were housed in triangular concrete prisms closed off from their surroundings, facing each other across an inner courtyard. The architect's sophisticated project description was illustrated by a set of eighteen large pencil drawings on tracing paper: twelve plans and axonometries of the buildings accompanied by six hand-drawn reproductions of references from art (Paul Klee, Henry Moore, Roy Lichtenstein, Walter De Maria, Sol LeWitt, Alfred Jensen) (fig. 7). On the exhibition panels and catalogue pages, this exquisite set of hand drawings is flattened to thumbnail-sized photocopies, nine per page. Reduced to stamp-sized conveyors of information, they demonstrate the architectural drawing's loss of agency when subjected to indiscriminate reproduction (fig. 8).

Beyond the violence of this reprographic process stands a perceptible means of rationalization, whereby the implacable grid mirrors the constructed unity of both curatorial selection and theoretical argument. A softer and more detailed gaze, which could have discussed buildings in terms of textures, hesitations, or extra-architectural circumstances, was substituted by a common layout that flattens their intrinsic diversity. It matters little that the architects, once selected, were actually given the choice to put forward their own selection of projects.[7] Their simmered-down presen-

7 See catalogue imprint: "Den eingeladenen Architekten wurde die Auswahl

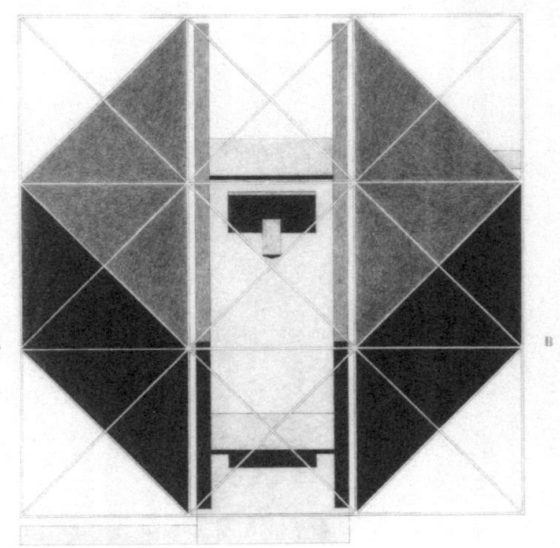

7   Giancarlo Durisch, drawing for the *Abitazione* (house) and *Studio* (atelier) in Riva San Vitale, 1974–75: *scema ordinatore delle misure e dei rapporti geometrici* (ordering diagram of measures and geometric relations). Pencil on paper, full-scale reproduction of original on tracing paper, ca. 55 × 40 cm

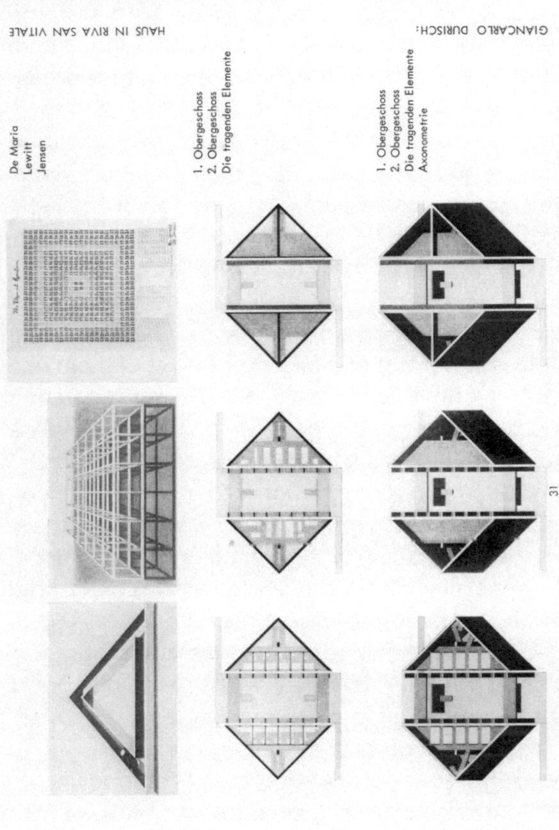

8 Giancarlo Durisch's reference drawings and axonometric plans of House and Atelier Durisch, Riva San Vitale, 1974–75, from the *Tendenzen* catalogue, 1975, p. 31. Here shown as maquette page in the pre-printing stage (on lithographic film)

tation reduced the impact of free agency. As a systematic classification of content, the *Tendenzen* catalogue became truly a *catalogue raisonné*. It epitomizes the production of discourse: the paper apparatus that engulfs the ideas, justifications, and theoretical contextualizations attached to existing built production, sustaining their presence in the architectural imagination and adding to the social and cultural capital of their authors.

Interestingly, this almost machine-like rigor is not intrinsic to the entire series of ETH Zurich exhibition catalogues at the time. While displaying similar graphic qualities and production values, in format and in content most of them reflect the intricacies of their own topic. Mediating between the space of architecture and that of the page, the *Tendenzen* catalogue exemplified a singularly systematic approach: the effort to fit the Ticinese production into a coherent theoretical reading, a square peg in a round hole. Was this reductive procedure the very cause for the exhibition's wider success? And more generally, is this succinct quality a precondition for generating architectural discourse?

The *Tendenzen* exhibition catalogue was neither a perfectly finished nor internally consistent piece of work. Despite—or maybe because of—its roughness, it proved remarkably resilient in terms of its mileage as an architectural publication. One suspects that its raw yet compelling quality was not only the result of its contents but also of what it had left out. The principles that governed the space of the catalogue's pages, made visible in the surviving maquette sheets, offer an unexpected glimpse into the intellectual framework of the exhibition. They reframed a heterogeneous series of 1960s and 1970s Ticinese projects so as to fit the unitary theoretical scaffold of architectural autonomy. The

der Werke freigestellt. Von dieser Möglichkeit haben Gebrauch gemacht: P. Brivio, T. Carloni, G. Durisch, D. Schnebli. Die übrigen Architekten haben die Wahl den Organisatoren überlassen," in Martin Steinmann and Thomas Boga, eds., *Tendenzen: Neuere Architektur im Tessin*, Second edition (Zurich: Organisationsstelle für Ausstellungen der Architekturabteilung an der ETH Zürich, 1976), 137.

archival collection of drawings, collages, and typewritten manuscripts that make up the catalogue maquettes thus testifies to the nature of the paper apparatus. The rereading and transposition of actual buildings into printed discourse involved an inevitable flattening: from space to page, from sensorial readings of the built environment to its intellectual analysis. The catalogue made manifest the structuring role of the space of the page, mediating between actual buildings and their representation in the space of the architecture exhibition. Using a concrete built production as primary evidence, its outcome was immaterial: the construction of discourse.

"RECENT" ARCHITECTURE IN TICINO

The interest surrounding Ticinese architecture in the mid-1970s coincided with a wider search for viable sequels to an exhausted modernism. In the late 1960s, Switzerland's long-established intellectual tradition of critical self-reflection collided with the provocative and expectant mood of the '68 generation.[8] At the time, Swiss architecture's alignment to modernism, unperturbed by wartime destruction and large-scale reconstruction, had reached oversaturation. In 1969, art historian Stanislaus von Moos commented dryly: "New directions in Swiss architecture? One is tempted to say: There are none."[9] For von Moos, postwar Switzerland presented a pragmatic and uninspiring "backyard of history," perhaps too caught up in its narrative of a prosperous democracy to foster genuine artistic debate. Its best hopes for a substantial architecture, he argued, lay in its unique status as "Europe's meeting place," both in terms of a historical orientation towards neighboring cultures and current possibilities of productive international exchanges.[10]

Von Moos's words proved prescient. It was in Ticino, a site of starker cultural encounters, that a "new direction in Swiss architecture" took shape. This incipient stage was first signaled by a collaborative entry to the federal competition for the polytechnic campus in Dorigny, Lausanne in 1970.[11] The master plan project, authored by Mario Botta, Aurelio Galfetti, Flora Ruchat-Roncati, Luigi Snozzi, and Tita Carloni under the moniker "Gruppo Ticino," located the emergence of a new collective voice (fig. 9). In contrast to the pragmatic zoning of other entries, it envisaged the new École polytechnique fédérale de Lausanne (EPFL) campus as a carpet-city, emphasizing its physical and historical connections to its

8 See Irina Davidovici, "The Background of Culture," in *Forms of Practice: German-Swiss Architecture 1980–2000* (Zurich: gta Verlag, 2012), 21–39.

9 Stanislaus von Moos, "New Directions in Swiss Architecture?," trans. Christian Casparis, in *New Directions in Swiss Architecture*, ed. Jul Bachman and Stanislaus von Moos (New York: Braziller, 1969), 11–40, here 11.

10 Moos, "New Directions in Swiss Architecture?" 13.

11 Botta, Mario, et al., *Scuola Politecnica Federale Losanna—Piano Direttore—Relazione* (Genestrerio: no publisher, 1970).

surroundings.[12] Set out to a northwest–southeast grid, the campus was structured by a raised walkway, an east–west *decumanus* connecting at its extremes a public transport hub and a natural leisure area. Along the perpendicular *cardo*, an axis of infrastructural buildings was oriented on the ground level towards the city and lakeshore. Weaving topographical and functional elements, the master plan nevertheless maintained its own formal cohesion in a geometrical composition extended to a territorial scale. The project's approach betrayed an interest in architectural autonomy aligned with contemporaneous theoretical debates in Italy.[13]

The project shared a set of urban strategies with the 1967 competition entry for the *bagno* (public bath) in Bellinzona, which two members of the collective, Galfetti and Ruchat-Roncati, realized together with Ivo Trümpy in 1970. Later described by Bruno Reichlin as a "paradigm of territorial architecture,"[14] this leisure complex of open-air swimming pools and sports facilities was likewise structured by a raised circulation spine, almost 300 meters long, allowing views of the mountains and physically connecting the city and the river Ticino (fig. 10). Both projects, in Dorigny and Bellinzona, similarly mediated between classical principles of urban planning and site-specific topographical and landscape features, intertwining monumental infrastructures with autonomous interventions at territorial, urban, and architectural scales.

Authored by overlapping, temporary collectives, both projects signaled the emergence of a recent Ticinese archi-

12 Cf. entries by the Arbeitsgruppe Zürich (pp. 647–50) and Gruppo Ticino (pp. 656–57) in Lucius Burckhardt and Diego Peverelli, "Sieben Projektaufträge für die ETH-L in Dorigny," *Das Werk: Architektur und Kunst / L'Oeuvre: Architecture et Art* 57, no. 10 (1970): 646–61.

13 See Laurent Stalder, "Verwaltete Architektur: Ein Rückblick auf die Jüngere Schweizer Baukunst," *Neue Zürcher Zeitung*, December 12, 2015, https://www.nzz.ch/feuilleton/kunst_architektur/verwaltete-architektur-1.18661562.

14 Bruno Reichlin, "Un paradigma di architettura territoriale," in *Il bagno di Bellinzona di Aurelio Galfetti, Flora Ruchat-Roncati, Ivo Trümpy*, ed. Nicola Navone and Bruno Reichlin (Mendrisio: Mendrisio Academy Press, 2010), 9–18, 9.

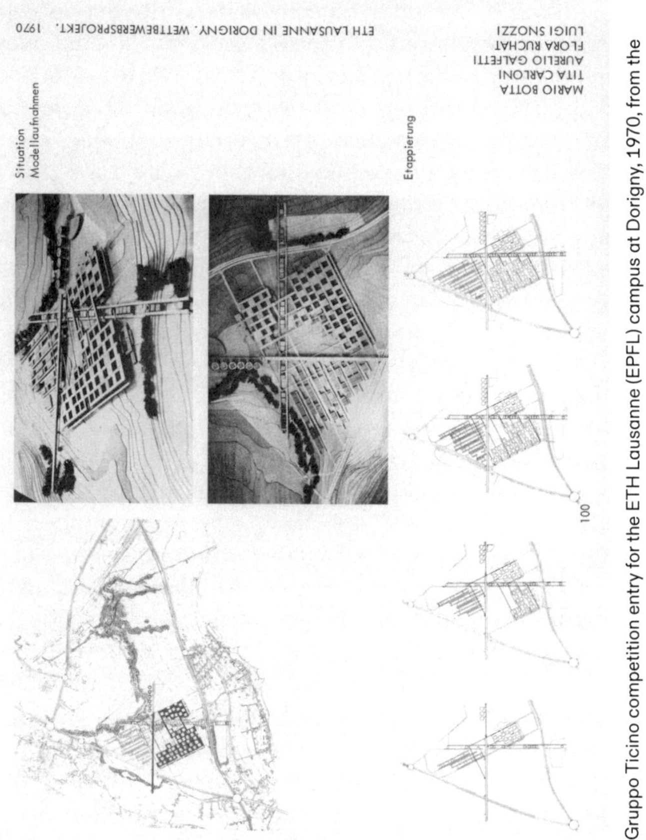

9   Gruppo Ticino competition entry for the ETH Lausanne (EPFL) campus at Dorigny, 1970, from the *Tendenzen* catalogue, 1975, p. 100

10 Aurelio Galfetti, Flora Ruchat-Roncati, Ivo Trümpy, public baths, Bellinzona, 1970. Part architectural, part landscape interventions, the baths represent an understanding of architecture as operating at territorial scale.

tecture as the confident intermediary between the Swiss architectural discourse and Italian readings of "typology," "history," "territory," and "form." These conceptual underpinnings were restated during a discussion, published in the journal *Werk*, between a group of Ticino architects and the editors Lucius Burckhardt and Diego Peverelli.[15] Ostensibly an assessment of the Banca della Svizzera Italiana in Lugano, a recently completed building by Giancarlo Durisch, the debate quickly moved to Ticino's urbanization. The published discussion revealed the extent to which this group of young architects were enthralled by the idea of the "city" expounded in Italian theory. Yet the architects' statements also acknowledged the tensions between the intellectual, artistic ambitions of their practice and the political visions of the rapidly developing Ticino as a pragmatic field of operations. With foresight, they emphasized the threatening impact of speculative development upon the canton's environment and cultural memory, in both its urban and rural contexts.

Highlighting a unique set of professional collaborations, the discussion also pinpointed the collectivist, territorial, and activist directions of this younger generation of Ticinese practitioners. This phenomenon was striking, especially when considering its parochial context. In a canton of less than three thousand square kilometers, with a quarter of a million inhabitants, their buildings were rooted in the still generally accepted tenets of modernism, and nevertheless subjected to local inflections.[16] The new works invited reflections on Ticino's status as an isolated cultural territory, split between

15 The discussion included the Ticinese architects Mario Botta, Tita Carloni, Aurelio Galfetti, Flora Ruchat-Roncati, Luigi Snozzi, and Giancarlo Durisch. Diego Peverelli and Lucius Burckhardt, eds., "Banca della Svizzera Italiana, Lugano," *Das Werk: Architektur und Kunst* 59, no. 1 (1972): 9–18.

16 See Gaudenz Risch, "Tendenzen: Neuere Architektur im Tessin," *Schweizerische Bauzeitung* 93, no. 50 (1975): 815–16.

its political allegiance to Switzerland and its historical, linguistically reinforced orientation towards Italy.[17]

Whereas up to the Second World War most Ticinese architects had been trained in Italy, the closure of the borders during the war permanently reversed this trend. While studying at ETH Zurich, the alternative training ground, younger generations had encountered the works of Le Corbusier, Frank Lloyd Wright, and Alvar Aalto. Building upon the diffusion of ideas of *Neues Bauen* in Ticino in the 1930s, these influences blended into a postwar modernism that came into its own in the 1950s, combining the local vernacular with "imported Germanic-Romantic interpretations."[18] By the early 1960s, as this generation of architects entered practice, "Ticinese Modernism" enjoyed a local status almost as self-evident as that of traditional architecture. Two of its most prominent protagonists, Rino Tami and Alberto Camenzind, were professors at ETH Zurich, where they mentored the younger generation at the centre of the 1970s debates.

This cultural trajectory attests to the existence of a strong generational self-understanding amongst Ticinese architects. While modernism continued to represent a stand against speculative development, the younger generation's allegiance to it was at once reflective and historicizing.[19] The projects of Galfetti, Ruchat-Roncati, and Snozzi recalled aspects of Le Corbusier's oeuvre; their mentor, Carloni, deferred to the work of Aalto and Wright. Botta's projects were formally influenced by Louis Kahn, Le Corbusier, and Carlo Scarpa, all of whom he had worked for while studying in Venice. Livio Vacchini's austere rationalism channeled Ludwig Mies van der Rohe and neo-plasticism. The geometrical experiments of Peppo Brivio and Durisch were indebted to

17 See Kenneth Frampton, "Mario Botta and the School of the Ticino," *Oppositions* 14 (1978): 1–25, here 3.

18 Risch, "Tendenzen," here 815.

19 See Martin Tschanz, "Tendenzen und Konstruktionen: Von 1968 bis heute," in *Architektur im 20. Jahrhundert*, ed. Anna Meseure, Martin Tschanz, and Wilfried Wang, vol. 5 (London: Prestel, 1998), 45–52, here 46.

Louis Kahn, while the Casa Tonini by Fabio Reinhart and Reichlin circumvented modernism altogether to embrace an abstracted Palladianism. In many of these projects, modernism was incorporated not as a mark of progress but itself as historical reference, on a par with vernacular patterns of dwelling, landscape, and settlement-making. Retrospectively, the synthesis of modernist and local motifs invited connotations with an "architecture of revolt" or "resistance," anticipating by a decade or more the narratives of critical regionalism.[20]

This production was neither stylistically nor qualitatively homogeneous. Its common features were rooted rather in a shared professional and cultural backdrop: a belief in the transformative potential of architecture, manifested through social and political engagement. Some of the architects openly criticized the environmental costs of rapid development in Ticino, while others adhered to left-wing political activism.[21] A second shared aspect was the strength of the local professional network. This often took the form of short-term, fluid partnerships between architects for the duration of a competition or series of projects. This collaborative mode of practice was organized along the architects' axes of teaching and training—between ETH Zurich and Italy—and conditioned by the cultural middle-ground in which they operated. Thirdly and crucially, the shared political and economic context of the postwar boom was particularly favorable to building. Ticino's expansion of manufacturing and services industries, its population growth, and its educational reform

20 See Dieter Bachmann and Gerardo Zanetti, eds., *Architektur des Aufbegehrens: Bauen im Tessin* (Basel: Birkhäuser, 1985).

21 Many of them held left-wing political views, and Luigi Snozzi and Tita Carloni were declared socialists. See Alberto Caruso, "Architettura e politica," *Archi: rivista svizzera di architettura, ingegneria e urbanistica / Schweizerische Zeitschrift für Architektur, Ingenieurwesen und Stadtplanung* 6 (2014): 47–48; Pietro Martinelli, "Tita Carloni architetto e uomo politico," *Archi: rivista svizzera di architettura, ingegneria e urbanistica / Schweizerische Zeitschrift für Architektur, Ingenieurwesen und Stadtplanung* 6 (2014): 50–53.

created the conditions allowing architectural experimentation to lead to actual construction.

Moreover, the rise in the number of middle-class professionals boosted the design of private houses for an educated clientele. This yielded a number of early gems, such as Botta's houses in Cadenazzo (1971) and Riva San Vitale (1972), Reichlin and Reinhart's Casa Tonini in Toricella (1974), and Durisch's own house and atelier in Riva San Vitale (1974). In parallel, the increase in the number of secondary school students in the late 1960s and early 1970s, and the resulting overhaul of Ticino's education system, led to the construction of an unprecedented number of new schools. Between 1971 and 1975, at least eight new educational buildings, for a total of six thousand students, were completed.[22] As public commissions awarded through public competitions, these projects helped architects move on from single-family houses. Botta's Liceo in Morbio Inferiore (1972–1976); the school complex in Riva San Vitale (1962–1972) by Galfetti, Ruchat-Roncati, and Trümpy; and the Scuola Media in Losone (1973), designed by Vacchini in collaboration with Galfetti are only a few examples.[23] A third category of new projects were the leisure and cultural facilities propelled by the bourgeoning tourism industry, of which the most important at the time were the public baths of Bellinzona (Galfetti, Ruchat-Roncati, Trümpy, 1967–1970)

22 See Redazione [Paolo Fumagalli and Peter Disch], "Architettura per la scuola: Le nuove scuole medie," pt. 1, *Rivista tecnica della Svizzera Italiana* 66, no. 10 (October 1975): 26–51, here 27.

23 To take only one segment of this extensive school-building program as an example, the new middle schools (for eleven- to fourteen-year-olds) were covered over three monthly issues of *Rivista Tecnica* at the end of 1975, with the journal not only reviewing the built projects but also reprinting excerpts from the main points of the reform published in the newspaper *Corriere del Ticino* on April 25, 1974. See Redazione [Paolo Fumagalli and Peter Disch], "Architettura per la scuola (part 1)"; Redazione [Paolo Fumagalli and Peter Disch], "Architettura per la scuola: Le nuove scuole medie," pt. 2, *Rivista tecnica della Svizzera Italiana* 66, no. 11 (November 1975): 28–57; Redazione [Paolo Fumagalli and Peter Disch], "Architettura per la scuola: Le nuove scuole medie," pt. 3, *Rivista tecnica della Svizzera Italiana* 66, no. 12 (December 1975): 19–46.

and the Castello Montebello Museum (Mario Campi, Franco Pessina, Niki Piazzoli, 1974), both in the cantonal capital.

Culturally, Ticino has long oscillated between Italy, its traditional next-of-kin, and the Swiss Confederation, its economic and administrative anchor. Its architecture reflected this double heritage in the juxtaposition of the local stone vernacular with modernist imports from Italy and Germany. This hybrid legacy was enriched, for the architects active in the 1960s and 1970s, by a number of other modernist allegiances, and particularly a collective devotion to Le Corbusier. Carloni, a prominent mentor of the younger generation, described its outlook as "entirely shaped within contemporary architecture, without explicit connections to the origins of modernism or a pre-industrial past."[24] The search for a suitable modernist vocabulary forged a generational self-understanding that explored a range of relationships with history. A collective identity arose from the training of most protagonists at ETH Zurich and was later nurtured in the studios of local masters such as Tita Carloni, Peppo Brivio, Franco Ponti, and Rino Tami. In this tight professional setting numerous architectural collaborations were instigated, some more durable than others. For instance, Reichlin and Reinhart, as well as Aurelio Galfetti, Flora Ruchat-Roncati, and Ivo Trümpy, gained fame in early partnerships before going separate ways. Moreover, Luigi Snozzi, Livio Vacchini, Mario Botta, and Galfetti (after his partnership with Ruchat-Roncati and Trümpy ended in 1970) became yet better known as sole practitioners, despite many of their earlier defining projects having been developed in collaborations. These fluid work alliances proved to have been highly circumstantial, rather than the manifestations of an ideologically motivated collectivism.

24 Tita Carloni, "Tra conservazione e innovazione: Appunti sull'architettura nel canton Ticino dal 1930 al 1980," in *50 anni di architettura in Ticino, 1930-1980: Quaderno della rivista tecnica della Svizzera Italiana*, ed. Peter Disch (Bellinzona-Lugano: Grassico Pubblicità, 1983), 4–11, here 9.

This tension between collective image and individual trajectories requires some unpacking. The aura of collectivism associated with this generation of Ticino practitioners is better explained as a dialectic of mutual and private interests, unfolding over time. On the one hand, the early pattern of working in groups extended in time the professional and social networks that the participants had developed as students, sometimes even earlier. For better or worse—for it had benefits as well as drawbacks—this condition reflected the provincial reality of a given socioeconomic group with a limited range of educational and professional options. On the other hand, the architects' individual careers developed at different speeds and branched out in different areas of activity, with varying degrees of commercial and academic success. This divergence of subsequent positions was not only based on circumstance but also, to some extent, revealed the architects' inherently varied agendas, priorities, and political convictions.

To some extent, this variety was reflected in the built projects, whose heterogeneity resisted, inconveniently for critics, a coherent reading as the manifestation of a single attitude. At a basic formal level, the buildings shared some stylistic affinities, for example for cubic volumes, barefaced concrete surfaces, abstracted vernacular forms, and sensitive relationing to the topography. Moreover, even in rural settings, the architectural ambition of cultural recovery generated a sense of fragmented urbanity.[25] Modernist, vernacular, even classical sources were used in a polemical and intellectualized fashion—not as a way of smoothing the prismatic architecture into its locale, but rather for highlighting its rootedness in a highbrow cultural tradition.

25 See Martin Steinmann, "La Scuola ticinese all'uscita da scuola," in *Il bagno di Bellinzona di Aurelio Galfetti, Flora Ruchat-Roncati, Ivo Trümpy*, ed. Nicola Navone and Bruno Reichlin (Mendrisio: Mendrisio Academy Press, 2010), 35–44; Paolo Fumagalli, "L'architettura degli anni Settanta nel Ticino," *Kunst+Architektur in der Schweiz / Art+Architecture en Suisse / Arte+Architettura in Svizzera* 46, no. 1 (1995): 28–35.

On an ideological front, however, this architecture remained remarkably quiet. Even though the leftist tendencies of several of its architects led to a declared interest in social practices and programs, such as housing, actual opportunities were few.[26] The architectural output largely depended on a regional economy of private middle-income residences, punctuated by historical refurbishments. The real chance for this production to claim a social dimension instead arose with the 1960s educational reform, which funded many new school buildings in Ticino and effectively launched many of these young architects' careers. It did not take long before the world of architecture turned its attention to this regional output, hailing it as a genuinely "new direction" in Swiss architecture (fig. 11).

26 For the cultural and political resistance to collective housing in the Ticino, as well as the 1970s architects' efforts to overcome it, see Paolo Fumagalli, "Il Collettivo in Ticino," *Archi: rivista svizzera di architettura, ingegneria e urbanistica / Schweizerische Zeitschrift für Architektur, Ingenieurwesen und Stadtplanung* 6 (2013): 65–71.

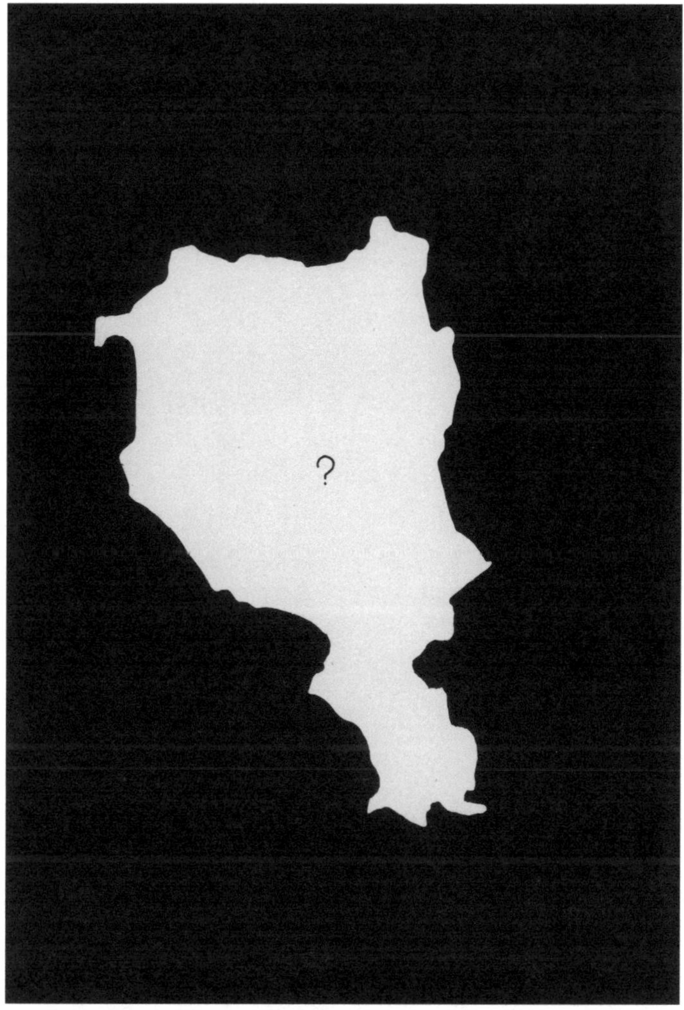

11 The frontispiece of the editorial to the 1973 *Rivista tecnica* issue *Contraddizioni di un territorio in espansione. Due esempi: vàlle Maggia e Lugano* (Contradictions of an expanding territory. Two examples: Maggia Valley and Lugano). The unattributed drawing was possibly made by Flora Ruchat-Roncati, one of the guest editors of this issue.

THE CURRENCY OF TENDENCY

The production of private houses, schools, and public buildings in Ticino in the 1970s was catalogued for the first time at ETH Zurich, the alma mater of many of the architects involved. The exhibition *Tendenzen: Neuere Architektur im Tessin* opened in Zurich on November 20, 1975, and closed—five days later than originally planned—on December 17 (fig. 12). This brief, rather modest event resonated surprisingly widely. It marked not only the beginning of the external critical reception of Ticinese architecture, but also a pivotal moment in the historiography of Swiss architecture, variously described by historians and critics as "legendary,"[27] "one of the most influential exhibitions for the generation of [Swiss] architects born around 1950,"[28] and "an important contribution to the discourse on realism."[29]

Curator Martin Steinmann reframed the "recent" Ticinese architecture as a site of knowledge transfers between Italy and northern Switzerland, placing it under the theoretical banner of the *Tendenza*. In hindsight, this event represents an important contribution to the design methodology that permeated Swiss architecture in the following decades. Its original and timely reading of architectural realism invited a focus on a close analysis of urban environments, the integration of historical and contextual references, and the formal and material gravitas of architectural objects. In the short course of the exhibition, however, this migration of ideas and methods was only made possible through the

27 Interview with Martin Steinmann, Karin Salm, "'Ich wollte Architekten zum Nachdenken über ihre Arbeit bringen'," *Schweizer Radio und Fernsehen (SRF)*, June 13, 2016, https://www.srf.ch/kultur/kunst/ich-wollte-architekten-zum-nachdenken-ueber-ihre-arbeit-bringen.

28 Ruth Hanisch and Steven Spier, "'History Is not the Past but Another Mightier Presence': The Founding of the Institute for the History and Theory of Architecture (gta) at the Eidgenössische Technische Hochschule (ETH) Zurich and Its Effects on Swiss Architecture," *The Journal of Architecture* 14, no. 6 (2009): 655–86, https://doi.org/10.1080/13602360903357096, here 668.

29 K. Michael Hays, introduction to Martin Steinmann, "Reality as History: Notes for a Discussion of Realism in Architecture," in *Architecture Theory since 1968*, ed. K. Michael Hays (Cambridge, MA: MIT Press, 1998), 246–53, here 246.

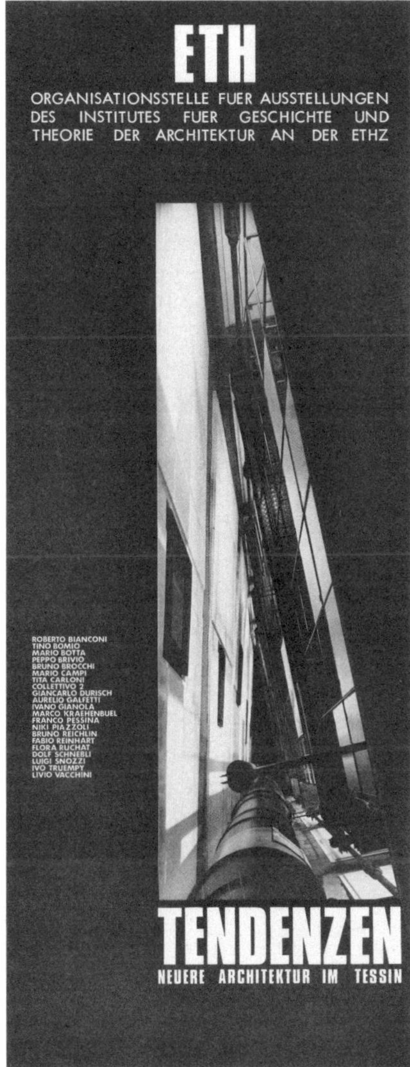

12 Exhibition poster for *Tendenzen: Neuere Architektur im Tessin*, ETH Zurich, 1975

sublimation of their historicity.[30] The Ticinese projects were de-situated—detached from the social, political, and economic particularities of their production—in order to resonate more widely at a disciplinary level. Paradoxically, even their self-definition in relation to their locale became one in a set of aesthetic criteria. Inner contradictions were glossed over as a way to project them more readily into the realm of theory.

The exhibition was organized by the ETH Zurich Department of Architecture's exhibitions program under the direction of Professor Heinz Ronner. According to Steinmann, Ronner had brought up the possibility of an exhibition on the young Ticinese on the evening of December 3, 1973, at the vernissage of the dual exhibition on Aldo Rossi and John Hejduk.[31] Steinmann, then a young architect and researcher at the Institute for the History and Theory of Architecture (gta Institute), recalled Ronner's wish to lend the same platform to the local phenomenon. "Now, it's the Ticinese's turn," was the sentiment of this initial discussion, if not the exact words. Steinmann was invited, then and there, to curate the future exhibition. The architect Thomas Boga, the permanent employee of the exhibitions program, was responsible for the production of displays and the catalogue.[32] And, although not frequently cited in relation to the exhibition, it is likely that Ronner remained personally involved—certainly in the early stages as the exhibition concept took shape, as well as in contributing to the catalogue.[33] In June 1975, presumably as part of the exhibition research, Steinmann recorded

30 See K. Michael Hays, "Introduction to Jean-Louis Cohen, 'The Italophiles at Work'," in *Architecture Theory since 1968*, ed. K. Michael Hays (Cambridge, MA: MIT Press, 1998), 506–521, here 506.

31 Steinmann in conversation with the author, Zurich, December 12, 2016.

32 The exhibition installation, catalogue production, and its subsequent re-hangings throughout Europe were coordinated by Thomas Boga; Steinmann was responsible for its intellectual content.

33 The gta Archive holds notes of preparatory meetings with Ticinese architect Luigi Snozzi dated December 11, 1973, and February 2, 1974 (handwritten by Ronner or Boga). At the time, Snozzi was teaching as a guest professor at ETH Zurich.

the Ticinese projects, some of them still in construction, in a series of slide films.

No photographs of the actual exhibition survive, leaving little possibility to reconstruct the original installation at the Globus Provisorium. The venue in the center of Zurich, designed by Karl Egender as a temporary location for the Globus department store in 1961, is itself not without interest. Having ceased operations in 1967, the Provisorium was the site of violent clashes between students and the police during the street riots of May 1968 before it was outsourced to ETH Zurich as temporary studio for its architecture students. At the time of the exhibition, in late 1975, the lease had almost expired. Nowadays, having long outlived its intended time span, the building is still in use as a supermarket and is the subject of public consultations as one of the city's most coveted sites for development. While it is difficult to imagine its earlier roles as an architecture studio and exhibition venue—let alone its revolutionary past—its use as a supermarket is telling of its generic and flexible interior.

Chances are that the exhibition itself was quite basic. According to the one surviving plan, the panels of *Tendenzen* were arranged in a loose, elongated U-shape figure in the lobby, on simple, self-standing partitions (fig. 13). The exhibit featured a total of forty-eight projects—mostly private houses, schools, and historical restorations—by twenty-one practices, laid out on sixty-six panels in a landscape format in size A0—approximately 90 × 120 centimeters. Graphically sparse, the black-and-white display panels showed the buildings in conventional architectural representations: plans, sections, photographs. Apart from the projects' authors, dates, and locations, on the panels there was minimal textual input, mostly leaving the graphic representations to speak for the architecture.

Conceptually, the *Tendenzen* exhibition was more than a regional survey of new buildings in one of Switzerland's peripheries. Instead, it framed Ticinese architecture as a

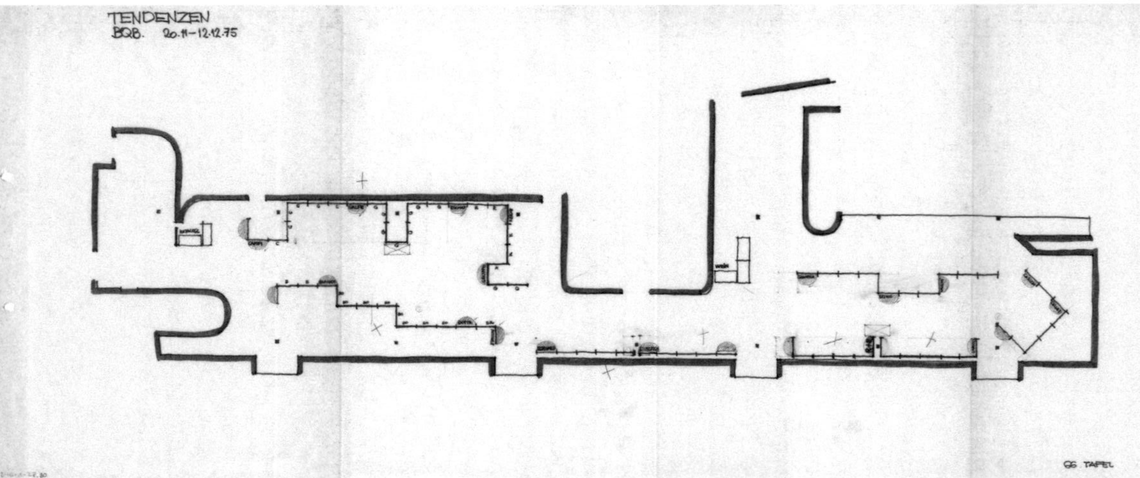

13 Plan layout of the *Tendenzen* exhibition in the Globus Provisorium. Felt-tip pen drawing on translucent paper, attributed to Thomas Boga

Swiss counterpart to the work of Aldo Rossi and his Italian contemporaries, or rather, as a built manifestation of their theories. Shortly after the end of Rossi's influential professorship at ETH Zurich between 1972 and 1974, together with the Ticinese Bruno Reichlin and Fabio Reinhart as assistants, the show was calibrated to help his audience process the momentous methodological discourse he had left behind.[34] The *Tendenzen* exhibition presented the architecture of Ticino as an exemplar of how the Italian *Tendenza* could be reconceived for the Swiss context. To this end, the organizers—assuming a certain political risk—snubbed Ticino's modernist establishment, represented at ETH Zurich by professors Rino Tami and Alberto Camenzind, and indeed the modernist mainstream of the ETH faculty as whole. Instead, Steinmann chose to focus on recent projects from the 1960s and early 1970s, which became—against his intention—largely subsumed under the theoretical framework of the Italian *Tendenza*. Tethered to the contemporaneous and ideologically appealing *Tendenza*, this architecture was implicitly framed as symptomatic of a generational shift (fig. 14). This reading was only partly true, as the protagonists, as much as Steinmann himself, were still deeply conditioned by the modernist architecture they had been exposed to during their training.

For a long time, the exhibition's provisional title remained simply *Die Tessiner*—The Ticinese. Steinmann's choice, *Neuere Architektur im Tessin* (Recent architecture in Ticino) received a last-minute addition from Ronner—one word that irrevocably changed its message and future reception. As Steinmann later recalled, "Ronner found that too unspectacular and suggested 'Tendenza' as a title. That was a reference to *Architettura Razionale* and the 15th Triennale of Milan curated by Aldo Rossi in 1973. The allusion was

---

34 For Rossi's influence at ETH Zurich, see Ákos Moravánszky and Judith Hopfengärtner, eds., *Aldo Rossi und die Schweiz: Architektonische Wechselwirkungen* (Zurich: gta Verlag, 2011).

Ausst. "Die Tessiner"   Snozzi 11.12.73

Die frühe Moderne i Tessin   ⌐ Chiattone
                                      ⌊ — ~~Tami~~

                              20/30 deutsche Flüchtlinge
                                 n ⌐ Felsenkampf
                                    ⌊ Weidemeier
                                      Segal

die mittl. Generation   ⌐ • Tami
                              4   ⌡ • Camenzind
                                   ⌊ • Jäggli

die neue Generation   ⌐ Carloni
                            28.8   │ Brivio   — ⋇ • ⌉3
                                   │ Fr. Ponti
                                   ├ Galfetti
                                   ├ Botta
                                   ├ Ruchat
Schnebli   ├ Snozzi
Pauli   │ Durisch ⌉
(Grisel)   4├ Vacchini │
(Dolhinden)   │ Gizmola ⌋ 2
(Studer)   ~~Fra Ponti~~
                                     Bianchoni

---

14 Notes of a preparatory meeting for the exhibition dated December 11, 1973,
    showing generational self-understanding of Ticinese architects as proposed by
    Luigi Snozzi.

too restrictive, because my exhibition dealt with a range of attitudes. So the title became *Tendenzen.*"[35] For Steinmann, the title "sought a false proximity to Rossi's *Tendenza*, even when put in the plural: *Tendenzen*. As far as I'm concerned, I've always spoken of 'recent architecture in Ticino,' a term that eludes all labels."[36]

The exhibition's final title is therefore a compromise between two contradictory aims. On the one hand, Steinmann had sought to establish a connection between Ticino's regional identity and its recent local architecture. On the other, the exhibition's title—in what could be seen as cunning marketing on Ronner's part—implied affinities between the Ticinese work and the Italian *Tendenza* discourse, which elicited the curiosity of the Northern Swiss audience. The negotiations resulted in the German plural form *Tendenzen*, which acknowledged the heterogeneity of the actual Ticinese production and its due to Italian theory, while at the same time establishing a necessary distance from it.

Offering a theoretical justification for the built works on display, the exhibition catalogue proved key to its long-term success by including all its panels reduced to the format of the book. In addition, the text sections allowed Steinmann, Ronner, Boga, and the Ticinese protagonists to build up an overarching textual argument, which both incorporated and complemented the laconic, disjointed visual material of the exhibition. The catalogue was organized in three parts. In the introductory section, two essays, by Ronner and Steinmann respectively, illustrate a somewhat stiff division between the history and the theory of the phenomenon at

35 Martin Steinmann and Daniel Kurz, "Experienced Space: Daniel Kurz in Conversation with Martin Steinmann," in *Prix Meret Oppenheim 2016: Adelina von Fürstenberg, Christian Philipp Müller, Martin Steinmann—Schweizer Grand Prix Kunst / Grand Prix suisse d'art / Gran Premio svizzero d'arte / Grond premi svizzer d'art* (Bern: Bundesamt für Kultur, 2016), 120.

36 Steinmann, "La Scuola ticinese," here 35. Originally delivered as the lecture "L'école tessinoise à la sortie des classes," on the occasion of the exhibition *Il Bagno di Bellinzona* vernissage at the Accademia di Architettura, Mendrisio, September 17, 2009.

hand. Ronner's essay, "Zur Lage der Architektur im Tessin" (On the Situation of Architecture in Ticino), aimed to situate the Ticinese production in the cultural and historical context of the local modernist tradition, highlighting its connections to the ETH discourse. Steinmann's essay conveyed a purely theoretical stance. His contribution prioritized the internal and historically generated laws of the discipline over the actual conditions of production. The paradox of architectural autonomy was seen as pivotal for understanding Ticinese production:

> One essential common denominator of these architects is their clear conception of the relationship of architecture to these mentioned conditions [existing hegemonies and ideologies], and also the recognition that architecture is a discipline which possesses its own internal laws; i.e. which is autonomous. … The meaning of architecture defines itself in relation to its own tradition … .[37]

This emphasis on autonomy helped Steinmann's argument cut across the territorial, cultural, and disciplinary indexes of the buildings. It framed instead a universal Western dilemma of creative endeavor, focused on architecture as a "problem of form," to adopt Snozzi's eloquent formulation. Steinmann also wrote about design and criticism as being "structurally related"—an equivalence that undermined the former's crystalline autonomy.[38] As he would later admit, "I wanted to have architects, who don't write, to at least speak out and expound their positions."[39] Indeed, the *Tendenzen* catalogue was the first of many publications in which Steinmann encouraged

37 Martin Steinmann, "Reality as History: Notes for a Discussion of Realism in Architecture," in *Tendenzen: Neuere Architektur im Tessin*, Second edition, ed. Martin Steinmann and Thomas Boga (Zurich: ETH Zurich, 1976), 155–57, here 155.

38 Steinmann 1976, in Hays, 252.

39 Steinmann and Kurz, "Experienced Space," 120. See also Salm, "'Ich wollte Architekten zum Nachdenken über ihre Arbeit bringen'."

practicing architects to stake out, in writing, their intellectual and methodological credentials. This occurred in the second section of the catalogue, "Contributions to Design," which featured nine projects from the exhibition accompanied by explanatory texts from their authors. Following this sequence of short texts, the buildings were presented in commentary-free format on pages identical to the exhibition panels. The projects were separated into programmatic categories: family houses, social housing, schools and nurseries, public buildings, and restorations. The final and most conventional section of the catalogue, containing biographies and lists of works, provides a revealing subtext, indicating that the majority of participants had studied, and often also taught, at ETH Zurich. The exhibition therefore did not present a significant "other" to the ETH audience; rather, it showed how its own culture could incorporate something new.

The section "Contributions to Design" highlighted a subtle hierarchization, giving a more prominent arena to a few emerging *auteurs*. The diversity of architects' voices to emerge from this exercise was telling of the plurality of their positions. Galfetti, Ruchat-Roncati, and Trümpy gave a dry, factual description of their Bellinzona public baths, which refrained from explicit aesthetic or ideological statements. Campi, Pessina, and Piazzoli's reluctance to commit to paper their method— presumably quite intuitive—for the Montebello Castle project, was also palpable: "we mean to point out the difficulties we have experience [sic] in expressing an architectural event with the analytical tools of the written word."[40] Conversely, other participants were clearly more at ease with these tools. Giancarlo Durisch situated his radical design for a house and studio in Riva San Vitale in a matrix of references to contemporary and modernist artworks by Paul Klee, Henry Moore, Roy Lichtenstein, Walter

---

40 Mario Campi, Franco Pessina, and Niki Piazzoli, "Montebello Castle in Bellinzona," in *Tendenzen: Neuere Architektur im Tessin*, Second edition, ed. Martin Steinmann and Thomas Boga (Zurich: ETH Zurich, 1976), 162.

De Maria, Sol LeWitt, and Alfred Jensen. His art-architecture analogies were based on his "conviction that every cognitive-creative process, in particular architectonic ones, is part of one intellectual sphere."[41] For their Tonini House, Reichlin and Reinhart developed a sophisticated *concetto* quoting literary sources as diverse as Edgar Allan Poe, Paul Valéry, Walter Benjamin, and Leon Battista Alberti.[42] Botta's text on the Morbio Inferiore gymnasium articulated a design method centered on anchoring the building in its location, seeking their symbiosis at cultural and topographical levels. He emphasized, with a rhetorical use of capital letters, that "the architectonic intervention does not provide the opportunity of building on a SITE but rather provides the tools for building THAT SITE."[43]

It was nevertheless Snozzi, reflecting upon his teaching experience at ETH Zurich, who provided the clearest didactic statement of method. In his text, he listed the principles deployed in design processes: the reference to architectural history; a critical reappraisal of *Neues Bauen*'s social ambitions; the study of city and territory as fields of architectural intervention; the reliance on typological and morphological analysis; and architecture's primary focus on the "problem of form":

The designer must approach the problems of architecture starting from form. Thus, other approaches (sociological, economic, etc.), which in recent years have provided architects with an avenue of escape from their true responsibilities, must be excluded. It is my

41 Giancarlo Durisch, "House in Riva San Vitale," in *Tendenzen: Neuere Architektur im Tessin*, Second edition, ed. Martin Steinmann and Thomas Boga (Zurich: ETH Zurich, 1976), 160–61, here 160.

42 Bruno Reichlin and Fabio Reinhart, "Two Houses," in *Tendenzen: Neuere Architektur im Tessin*, Second edition, ed. Martin Steinmann and Thomas Boga (Zurich: ETH Zurich, 1976), 163.

43 Mario Botta, "Academic High School in Morbio Inferiore: Intervention Criteria and Design Objectives," in *Tendenzen: Neuere Architektur im Tessin*, Second edition, ed. Martin Steinmann and Thomas Boga (Zurich: ETH Zurich, 1976), 160.

contention that the failure of the architect in contemporary interdisciplinary work is due mainly to his lack of depth in his own discipline.[44]

Snozzi thus implicitly criticized the dominance of sociological studies in ETH teaching during the 1960s and early 1970s. Intended as a corrective to this polemical conceptual climate, this position was aligned to the methodological agenda articulated by Aldo Rossi during his recent post at ETH Zurich.[45]

This belief that architectural design followed its own intrinsic rules manifested itself in the lack of curatorial interest in the specific historical, political, and technological contexts of the built Ticinese production. Overall, and despite Ronner's introduction, the catalogue made little effort to situate the work against the background of practice. The astonishing fact that a handful of young, unproven practitioners had gained—mostly in competition—such access to public commissions was not made explicit. Neither was the cantonal program for the construction of educational buildings in the late 1960s and early 1970s, through which most of the public projects had been commissioned, even mentioned. The contradiction between the architecture's socially transformative aims and its actual conditions, favorable at best to individual experiments with middle-class villas, was never highlighted. Such commentaries would only arise later, in the mid-eighties, after the formal furor had abated—and even then, as we later see, from local actors rather than out-

44 Luigi Snozzi, "Design Motivation," in *Tendenzen: Neuere Architektur im Tessin*, Second edition, ed. Martin Steinmann and Thomas Boga (Zurich: ETH Zurich, 1976), 164. This emphasis on the autonomy of architecture, as opposed to other forms of knowledge, would have a considerable impact on ETH teaching through the longer-term involvement of Ticinese actors as visiting and permanent professors at ETH Zurich, including some of the original protagonists of the *Tendenzen* exhibition: Fabio Reinhart, Dolf Schnebli, Flora Ruchat-Roncati, and Mario Campi.

45 For Rossi's influence on teaching at ETH Zurich, see Hanisch and Spier, "'History Is not the Past'," 659–667; Moravánszky and Hopfengärtner, *Aldo Rossi und die Schweiz*; Irina Davidovici, *Forms of Practice: German Swiss Architecture, 1980–2000* (Zurich: gta Verlag, 2012), 52–66.

siders, and from literary critics and historians rather than architects.[46]

From the start, the show enjoyed remarkable success, with Ticino architecture swiftly claimed as representative of the wider Swiss discourse. An early reviewer in the *Schweizerische Bauzeitung* commented that "the imaginative, independent architecture of our Ticino colleagues, currently working individually and in groups, has for once been valued by the exhibition in Zurich, not only as a contribution to the discussion, but also as part of Swiss architecture."[47] Prompt remountings in Lausanne and Bellinzona in 1976 confirmed this wider interest and inaugurated a decade of traveling installations in venues including Basel, Munich, Karlsruhe, Innsbruck, Vienna, Salzburg, and Barcelona. (A US tour, though discussed, never materialized.) The same early review encouraged the public to "please refer to the catalog, in which the exhibition material is documented *in full [vollständig]*, with introductory and explanatory texts."[48] Its emphasis on *full* in italics is worth noting: the exhibition's circulation was dwarfed by that of its catalogue, whose repeated print runs grew from the 500 copies of the first edition (1975) to the 738 of the second (1976), and 1,500 copies of the third edition (1977). A facsimile reprint of a further 1,500 copies, published by Birkhäuser thirty-five years after the original, is still in print.

From the second edition onwards, the catalogue featured Italian and English versions of all texts, which had originally been published in German. The addition of translations (or in some cases the Italian texts in original) is illustrative of the international interest later confirmed by many publications. Already in the summer of 1976, *a+u* editor Toshio Nakamura organized a thematic issue on Ticino private houses, featuring texts and projects directly trans-

46 See, for example, Dieter Bachmann, "Gründer, Schüler, Epigonen," *Du: Die Zeitschrift für Kunst und Kultur* 546 (August 1986): 66–72, especially page 67.

47 Risch, "Tendenzen," 815.

48 Risch, "Tendenzen."

posed from the exhibition (fig. 15).[49] A year later, a smaller selection from the same projects was republished in the *Formalisme—Réalisme* issue of *L'architecture d'aujourd'hui*, edited by Bernard Huet under the heading "La 'tendenza' dans le Tessin"[50] (fig. 16). Notably, Huet disregarded the rather subtle plural of the exhibition title, simplifying the more nuanced relation between the southern Swiss production and its Italian undercurrents to the point of equivalence. He was not alone in doing so. Kenneth Frampton's 1978 article "Mario Botta and the School of the Ticino" cemented the hypothesis of a comprehensive built production with a unitary theoretical and ideological basis—a premise whose consequences will be examined later.[51] Through international channels, the "recent" Ticinese architecture became a global brand, promoted in high-profile publications, exhibitions, and architectural tours throughout the 1980s and beyond.

The attention that this new Ticinese phenomenon garnered was not all positive. Huet's *Formalisme—Réalisme* anthology included a rather tetchy review of the *Tendenzen* exhibition by Italian critic Francesco Dal Co, who also overlooked the curators' admittedly subtle demarcation of the German plural *Tendenzen* from the Italian form in singular, *Tendenza*.[52] Dal Co bemoaned the term's transposition to a provincial cultural context, warning against its "debasement" through overuse.[53] He first aimed his critical salves at the Ticinese buildings themselves, which he saw as no more than a "conscientious interpretation" of Le Corbusier and Aldo Rossi. From this, he concluded that the exhibition's curatorial angle opened "a blatant gap between reality and

<hr>

49 "Residences," *a+u / Architecture and Urbanism* 69 (September 1976): 23–145.

50 Bernard Huet, ed., "La 'tendenza,' ou l'architecture de la raison comme architecture de tendance," *L'architecture d'aujourd'hui* 190 (1977): 47–70.

51 Frampton, "Mario Botta."

52 Francesco Dal Co, "Critique d'une exposition," *L'architecture d'aujourd'hui* 190 (1977): 58–60.

53 Dal Co, "Critique d'une exposition," 58.

15 Cover of *a+u: Architecture and Urbanism* 69 (1976), edited by Toshio Nakamura, showing the interior of Casa Tonini in Torricella by Bruno Reichlin and Fabio Reinhart (1972–74). The issue published a selection of the single-family houses featured in the *Tendenzen* exhibition and English and Japanese translations of an extended version of Martin Steinmann's essay in the *Tendenzen* catalogue.

16   Cover of *L'Architecture d'aujourd'hui* 190 (April 1977), *Formalisme–Réalisme*, edited by Bernard Huet, with a drawing by Massimo Scolari. The issue, containing Francesco Dal Co's review of the *Tendenzen* exhibition alongside the response of Bruno Reichlin and Martin Steinmann, cemented the association between Ticinese architecture and the Italian *Tendenza*.

its 'representation.'"[54] In their response, running underneath Dal Co's text on the same pages, Steinmann and Reichlin elegantly rebuffed: "dans la nuit de la critique, tous les chats sont noirs"—in the night of critique, all cats are black.[55]

To be sure, Dal Co's negative reaction might have been borne of the frustration that the Italian theorizing practitioners had themselves fewer opportunities to build. Yet he did have a point, inasmuch as a tremendous effort had been made to inscribe all the Ticinese projects, despite marked differences of approach, within the unifying intellectual framework of the exhibition. In the "night of theory," the Ticinese projects became the "black cats" as shadowy reflections of the Italian discourse. Under the strain of this perceived distance between "reality and its representation," the unified theoretical interpretation peeled off from the declared intentions and varied influences of the built architecture.[56]

At its time, the *Tendenzen* exhibition outlined critical boundaries between Switzerland's culturally distinct regions, between the practice and criticism of architecture, and between its concrete embodiments and their representation in text and images. To be sure, the attempt to bring this architecture under one identifiable banner would be as futile as trying to subsume the plurality of the Ticinese *Tendenzen* under a single intellectual format. However, one should not underestimate the power of theoretical production to conceptualize a more complex reality into seductive, easily digestible interpretations. Rather, the exhibition and its theoretical justification signaled the first instance of the "Ticino

54 Dal Co, "Critique d'une exposition," 58–59.

55 Martin Steinmann and Bruno Reichlin, "Critique d'une critique," *L'architecture d'aujourd'hui* 190 (1977): 58–60, here 59.

56 The works of Galfetti, Ruchat-Roncati, Trümpy, and Snozzi had strong Corbusian overtones; Carloni and Collettivo 2 channelled Frank Lloyd Wright; Botta, Kahn and Scarpa; and Vacchini, Mies van der Rohe. Brivio's mannerism balanced Reichlin's and Reinhart's abstract Palladianism and the Terragni-inspired *razionalismo* of Mario Campi and Franco Pessina.

school" myth, which subsequent critical reinterpretations only consolidated.

With its emphasis on the formal and methodological aspects of the architecture, the *Tendenzen* exhibition largely overlooked the positions and ideological agendas of the buildings and practices it featured.[57] Thus, the Ticino practitioners' political concern with architecture's role in transforming society, their sense of social engagement, and their collaborative practices were overshadowed by the theoretical explanation of an aesthetic phenomenon.[58] Through its theoretical *topos*, the exhibition contrasted the cultural periphery of the architects' practice with the locations of architectural discourses in Zurich, Milan, and Venice. In establishing a connection with the Italian *Tendenza*, it oriented itself towards an international audience—acknowledging the currency of tendency, while at the same time distancing itself from it.

57 See Tschanz, "Tendenzen und Konstruktionen: Von 1968 bis heute," 46; Fumagalli, "L'architettura degli anni Settanta nel Ticino," 32.

58 Carloni and Snozzi, both members of the Partito Socialista Autonomo, were explicitly on the left of the political spectrum, with Snozzi making this part of his architectural "brand" (cf. Bachmann, "Gründer, Schüler, Epigonen," 67). Other contemporaries' political positions were more implicit—generally left-leaning, although with notable exceptions.

THE EMANCIPATION OF THEORY

Generally speaking, architectural exhibitions embody a transitional stage in the production of discourse, mediating between buildings and theory through graphic reproductions and textual interpretations. In the *Tendenzen* exhibition, the fluid sequence of built, graphic, and written materials emphasized Ticino's intermediary status as a "frontier-culture" between Italy and German-speaking Switzerland.[59] Itself justified by the import of Italian theory into Swiss building, the exhibition set into motion further transfers between built architecture and theoretical discourse. Three stages of such transfers can be identified. The first, prior to the exhibition (from circa 1965 to 1975), comprised the (partial) absorption of Italian *Tendenza* theory into the built production of the Ticino. The second stage (circa 1975 to 1978) took place at the time of the exhibition and shortly afterwards, as the new Ticinese architecture formed the basis for an increasingly autonomous theoretical narrative, in turn contributing to international debates around realism. The third stage (circa 1978 to 1986) represents the reabsorption of this body of realist theory into the built production of German-Swiss architecture and beyond. This occurred through its reformulation as a general design method, detached from the socioeconomic and cultural preconditions of 1970s Ticino.

Tendenzen invoked the connection between Ticino architecture and the theoretical discourse of the Italian *Tendenza*, already familiar to the Northern Swiss audience thanks to Aldo Rossi's teaching at ETH Zurich. Rossi had first postulated the notion in 1969 in the seminal text "L'architettura della ragione come architettura di tendenza" (Regional architecture as an architecture of tendency), written in the context of the exhibition *Illuminismo e architettura del settecento Veneto* (Illuminism and the architecture of eighteenth-century Veneto).[60] In this essay, Rossi defined *tendenza* as a shared stylistic will—"*volontà di stile*"—which he identified

<hr>

59 Frampton, "Mario Botta," 3.
60 Aldo Rossi, "L'architettura della ragione come architettura di tendenza," in

in the production of eighteenth-century Veneto artists and architects. For Rossi, stylistic will offered the possibility

> to analyse forms and the world of forms so as to arrive at an autonomous construct. This conception of art as pure speculation on appearance, as research into the existent forms of architecture, opens one of the most important avenues of modern art. Moreover, this combination of architectural objects, forms, materials is meant to create a potential reality of unexpected developments, to bring up different solutions, to construct the real.[61]

The historical and indeed regional circumstances of this occurrence mattered little to Rossi, who moved freely between historical commentary and theoretical proposition. The text explored the notion of *tendenza* as a perennial condition, with potential applicability in understanding and cataloguing contemporary work. The term itself had already been in circulation in the context of the *Casabella* journal's editorial team, which constituted a formative influence on Rossi. Ernesto Rogers had used it in a 1946 *Domus* article, which he later revisited in the essay "Elogio della tendenza" in 1958.[62] In this original sense, *tendenza* was primarily associated with the cultivation of historical conscience. For an artist's oeuvre to be coherent, Rogers argued, it needed to circumscribe a defined intellectual position, supported by a consistent cultural and moral horizon. To be relevant and truly critical, *Tendenza* delineated a deliberate pursuit of continuity by mediating between a personal artistic enterprise and the cultural context with which it had to engage. "To speak of

Illuminismo e architettura del '700 Veneto, Exhibition catalog: August 31–November 9, 1969, Palazzo del Monte, Castelfranco Veneto, ed. Manlio Brusatin, 1969, 7–15.

61 Rossi, "L'architettura della ragione," 9.

62 Ernesto Nathan Rogers, "Elogio della tendenza," in *Esperienza dell'architettura* (Turin: Einaudi, 1958), 124–126. Republished in *Esperienza dell'architettura* (Milan: Skira, 1997), 88–90.

tendenza," Rogers concluded, "is an act of modesty that integrates the activity of each individual into the culture of their epoch and leads them to consider themselves as being a part of society, which uses of the work of each individual to create history and represent it through styles."[63]

Twenty years later, by repositioning *tendenza* as *volontà di stile*, or "stylistic will," Rossi associated it more directly with the formal aspects of architecture. During the early 1970s, the notion settled into the more specific use and widespread form of *la Tendenza*—with a capital T. Coupled with the definite article, it morphed into a historical artistic movement, primarily associated with the abstract typological forays of neo-rationalist northern Italian architects—of Rossi, Vittorio Gregotti, Giorgio Grassi, and Massimo Scolari. This programmatic platform was thematized in the International Architecture section of the XV Milan Triennale in 1973, which Rossi curated. In the course of this exhibition, the meaning of *Tendenza* became firmly associated with the project of architectural autonomy. As defined by Scolari:

> For the Tendenza, architecture is a cognitive process that in and of itself, in the acknowledgment of its own autonomy, is today necessitating a refounding of the discipline; that refuses interdisciplinary solutions to its own crisis; that does not pursue and immerse itself in political, economic, social, and technological events only to mask its own creative and formal sterility, but rather desires to understand them so as to be able to intervene in them with lucidity.[64]

To be sure, the Swiss association with the Italian *Tendenza* went back further than Rossi's teaching at ETH Zurich in the early 1970s. It was in fact forged in the mid- to late 1960s in

63 Rogers, "Elogio della tendenza," 126.
64 Massimo Scolari, "The New Architecture and the Avant-Garde," in *Architecture Theory since 1968*, ed. K. Michael Hays (Cambridge, MA: MIT Press, 1998), 124–45, here 131–32.

the Ticino, through the shared language, geographical proximity, and the participation of some Ticinese protagonists in the Italian intellectual and professional milieu.[65] The plural in the title of the ETH exhibition, indicating the heterogeneity of formal vocabularies and ideological approaches in Ticinese architecture, was also a convenient shorthand, claiming for the Swiss participants some of the intellectual and ideological credentials of the Italian discourse. Parallels could be more clearly drawn in theory, such as Steinmann's attempt to filter the variegated Ticinese production through the prism of architectural autonomy. The *Tendenza* design principles, formulated by Scolari as "the strict relationship to history, the predominance of urban studies, the relation between building typology and urban morphology, monumentality, and the importance of form,"[66] reemerged almost unchanged in Luigi Snozzi's "points of reference" for design:

    a. Reference to history;
    b. Reference to the "New architecture" [*Neues Bauen*] as the last unifying element in architectural history … ;
    c. The analytical study of the city in all its topographical, historical and formal components;
    d. The study of typology and morphology.[67]

Steinmann's essay "Reality as History: Notes for a Discussion of Realism in Architecture" was calibrated to transcend the local situation and invited a purely theoretical stance (fig. 17). This strategy bestowed upon it a somewhat rarefied

---

65 Botta studied architecture at the Istituto Universitario di Architettura in Venice (IUAV), graduating in 1969. Reichlin taught at the Università degli Studi di Firenze as an assistant to Giovanni Klaus Koenig between 1969 and 1970. In Florence, Reichlin was exposed to architectural semiology, which he then taught at ETH Zurich after 1972. For their respective biographical details, see Martin Steinmann and Thomas Boga, eds., *Tendenzen: Neuere Architektur im Tessin / Tendencies: Recent Architecture in Ticino / Tendenze: Architettura recente nel Ticino*, Reprint of the third [1977] edition (Basel: Birkhäuser, 2010), 111, 130.

66 Scolari, "The New Architecture," 139.

67 Snozzi, "Design Motivation."

status, later confirmed by its high-profile translations and republications—as revised and expanded in *a+u / Architecture and Urbanism* in 1976, and as included in K. Michael Hays's 1998 anthology *Architecture Theory since 1968*.[68] The relevance of this text for international publications was reinforced precisely through its freedom vis-à-vis specific historical conditions. Rather than examining the development of the Ticinese works in the fullness of their actual context, Steinmann used them to punctuate a more general reflection on the nature of architectural reality.[69] As such, cultural and territorial particularities were minimized. Even the frequent references that implied Italian protagonists, such as Rogers and Rossi, were lost among the multiplicity of other sources from art and literature, including Bertolt Brecht, Edgar Allan Poe, Arnold Hauser, Le Corbusier, Roy Lichtenstein, and Peter Handke.

Steinmann's theoretical statement thus transgressed the territorial, cultural, and disciplinary context of the Ticino, or indeed Switzerland, to be more widely framed as a Western dilemma of creative endeavor. His approach promoted a dialectical autonomy, whereby the discipline prioritized its own internal, historically generated laws over the conditions of its production.[70] Architecture was rational, Steinmann contended, inasmuch as it defined itself in relation to its own traditions and techniques. This "autoreflexivity" guaranteed its cultural intelligibility: "If architecture makes reference to itself in this way, then history … is not merely a vast depository of experiences already made, but is rather the place where the meaning of architecture defines itself."[71] Instead of generating new meaning, or abandoning meaning altogether,

68 Martin Steinmann, "Reality as History: Notes for a Discussion of Realism in Architecture," *a+u* 69 (September 1976): 31–34; Steinmann, "Reality as History [1998]."

69 See K. Michael Hays, ed., *Architecture Theory since 1968* (Cambridge, MA: MIT Press, 1998), 246–253.

70 Snozzi, "Design Motivation."

71 Steinmann, "Reality as History [1998]," 249.

Wirklichkeit als Geschichte
(Stichworte ~~zur Frage der~~ *zu einem Gespräch über* Realismus in der Architektur)

"Heute, beklagte sich Herr K., gibt es Unzählige, die sich rüh-
men, ganz allein grosse Bücher verfassen zu können, und dies
wird allgemein gebilligt. (...) ~~Freilich gibt es dann auch kei-
nen Gedanken, der übernommen werden und auch keine Formulie-
rung eines Gedankens, die zitiert werden könnte.~~ Wie wenig brau-
chen diese alle zu ihrer Tätigkeit! Eine Feder~~halter~~ und etwas
Papier ist das einzige, was sie vorzeigen können! Und ohne Hilfe,
nur mit dem kümmerlichen Material, das ein einzelner auf seinen
Armen herbeischaffen kann, errichten sie ihre Hütten! Grössere
Gebäude kennen sie nicht als solche, die ein einzelner zu bauen
imstande ist!"
Bert Brecht: Geschichten vom Herrn Keuner

Architektur ist aus Gründen, die auf der Hand liegen, in beson-
derem Mass den herrschenden Kräften unterworfen und den herrschenden Begriffen, die Benjamin einmal die Spiegel eines Kalei-
doskopes nannte, dank denen immer wieder das Bild einer Ordnung
zustande kommt.
Die Frage, wieweit die Architektur unter diesen Bedingungen am
Kampf um die Veränderung der Gesellschaft teilhat, bildet den
Kern eines im "Werk" veröffentlichten Gespräches unter mehreren
an der Ausstellung beteiligten Architekten. Die klare Vorstel-
lung über das Verhältnis, in dem die Architektur zu diesen
äusseren Bedingungen steht, aber auch die Anerkennung von Architektur als einer Disziplin, die ihre eigenen inneren Gesetze be-
sitzt die mit anderen Worten autonom ist, bilden meiner Meinung
nach einen wesentlichen gemeinsamen Nenner dieser Architekten.

17   Martin Steinmann, annotated draft for the essay "Wirklichkeit als Geschichte"
(Reality as history), 1975, before publication in the *Tendenzen* catalogue

Steinmann suggested that the architect builds upon historically established associations to integrate the design into its cultural setting.

At the center of this argument stood the notion of *"répétition différente,"* an artistic procedure through which the architectural intervention is attached to a typological or morphological tradition, while simultaneously communicating its own "historicity."[72] The use of French in Steinmann's formulation acknowledged a debt to Gilles Deleuze's *Difference and Répétition* (1968), a philosophical reflection on the nature of reality. Deleuze saw "repetition" as the intellectual interaction between virtual and concrete aspects of reality; "difference" was, by default, intrinsic to repetition. A philosophy of repetition, according to Deleuze, was based on the injunction to "make something new of repetition itself: connect it with a test, with a selection or selective test; make it the supreme object of the will and of freedom.""[73] Paraphrasing Søren Kierkegaard, Deleuze positioned this movement of reinterpretation as a contemplative act: "Only contemplation of the mind which contemplates from without 'extracts'. It is rather a matter of acting, of making repetitions as such a novelty; that is, a freedom and a task of freedom."[74]

Outside of the Deleuzian frame, the interpretation of these principles slips very quickly into a hall of mirrors, bringing together historical precedent and creative gesture in the act of mimesis. In the Italian context, the role of repetition in design processes had been already theorized by Rogers in the 1950s. For him, repetition could help secure the intelligibility of architecture, its continuity within culture. In Rogers's continuity index, repetition was a creative act—a "dynamic continuation rather than passive copying."[75] Similarly, Rossi later understood the *tendenza* of eighteenth-century Veneto

72 Steinmann, "Reality as History [1998]," 252.
73 Gilles Deleuze, *Difference and Repetition*, trans. Paul Patton (London: Bloomsbury, 2014), 7.
74 Deleuze, *Difference and Repetition*, 7.
75 Ernesto Nathan Rogers, "Continuità," in *Esperienza dell'architettura* (Turin:

also in terms of a creative repetition: a "mixture of description and deformation, of invention and knowledge."[76]

Steinmann's *Tendenzen* theoretical construct was not exclusively about autonomy. It connected rationalism and history to the theme of architectural realism, reprised the following year in the issue of *archithese* titled "Realismus in der Architektur" coedited with Bruno Reichlin (fig. 18).[77] Their leading article argued that realism implied an empirical understanding of architecture: its ultimate aim was to be constructed and enjoyed in a material sense.[78] The emphasis on built projects in the *Tendenzen* exhibition a few months earlier can be understood in the same sense. It was guided by the conviction that the "inherent reality," on the terms of architecture's own traditions, was sufficient to ensure its integration into the surrounding culture. In the same issue of *archithese*, Steinmann and Reichlin invited Rossi to comment on the notion of realism in architecture. Rossi's text turned out to be surprisingly skeptical, colored by a clear distaste for the institutionalization of neo-realism in Italy, and as such it questioned the extent to which architecture, as opposed to literature and film, could reflect reality.[79]

Steinmann's notion of architectural realism can itself be seen as a *"répétition différente"* of the theoretical field developed by Rogers, Rossi, and Scolari, as well as its adoption by Reichlin, Rossi's assistant at ETH Zurich and arguably the

Einaudi, 1958), 130–133, here 131. The text was originally published in *Casabella-Continuità* 199 (January, 1954).

76 Rossi, "L'architettura della ragione," 7.

77 See Irina Davidovici, "Issues of Realism: Archithese, Postmodernism and Swiss Architecture, 1971–1986," in *Mediated Messages: Periodicals, Exhibitions and the Shaping of Postmodern Architecture*, ed. Véronique Patteeuw and Léa-Catherine Szacka (London: Bloomsbury Visual Arts, 2018), 101–20, https://doi.org/10.5040/9781350046207.

78 Bruno Reichlin and Martin Steinmann, "Zum Problem der innenarchitektonischen Wirklichkeit," *archithese* 19 (1976): 3–11.

79 Aldo Rossi, "Une éducation réaliste," *archithese* 19 (1976): 25–26. See further Bruno Reichlin, "Figures of Neorealism in Italian Architecture (Part 1)," trans. Antony Shugaar and Branden W. Joseph, *Grey Room* 6, no. 5 (2001): 78–101, particularly pp. 82–83.

Bruno Reichlin und Martin Steinmann

Zum Problem der innerarchitektonischen Wirklichkeit

«Wie Schiffer sind wir, die ihr Schiff auf offener See umbauen müssen, ohne es jemals in einem Dock zerlegen und aus besten Bestandteilen neu errichten zu können.»

Otto Neurath

Als um 1950 der Sozialistische Realismus (der als Theorie oder Methode in der Zeit vor dem Zweiten Weltkrieg ausgearbeitet worden war) mit seiner Auslegung den Begriff mit Beschlag belegte, wurde verschiedentlich versucht, ihm gerade von einem materialistischen Standpunkt aus das Neue Bauen als realistisch entgegenzustellen. Das gilt beispielsweise für Georg Schmidt, für den sich diese Auffassung darin bestätigte, dass «Sachlichkeit» das deutsche Wort für «Realismus» ist *(Realismus und Naturalismus)*. Der Satz seines Bruders Hans Schmidt, demzufolge Bauen seinem Wesen nach Technik, also eine Sache des Notwendigen sei, beschreibt die Grundlage dieses Realismus: Bauen sei Technik, die

«überall dort, wo sie keine wesensfremden Rücksichten zu nehmen hat, ein (. . .) *Rechnen mit bestimmten Gesetzen*, den Gesetzen der Kräfte, die in der Natur wirksam sind» *(Die Technik baut*, 1930).

Dieser Realismus richtet sich darauf, die Regeln des Stils oder allgemeiner der Form gegen «natürlichere» Gesetze (eben die Gesetze der Natur), auszutauschen, mit denen die Wirklichkeit unmittelbar zu erfassen wäre. (Im Rahmen dieses Heftes behandelt Alan Colquhoun diese Frage ausführlicher.)

(Es bezeichnet den Ernst seiner Auffassung, dass Hans Schmidt nach der Wirtschaftskrise die Formen des Neuen Bauens unter den veränderten Bedingungen der Produktion zeitweise

Au sujet de la réalité immanente de l'architecture

En architecture comme dans les arts en général la question du réalisme est d'habitude posée au niveau de la fonction expressive d'un œuvre qui, elle, n'existe qu'en relation avec une réalité *autre* que celle de l'architecture: les conditions matérielles et techniques, le système de production, la fonction sociale ou l'idéologie.

Cette idée de la réalité n'arrive pas à reconnaître dans les œuvres le travail qui les a produit. Mais si l'on néglige ce travail qui se réalise en elles, elles se présentent dans une «naturalité» illusoire, ne disant rien sur les processus qui déterminent le fonctionnement du fait poétique. Comme les autres arts, l'architecture ne reflète pas uniquement une réalité sociale. Elle possède sa propre réalité, qui est de nature formelle. D'où le postulat d'une théorie immanente à l'architecture, qui élabore des catégories capables d'identifier les méthodes poétiques réalisées dans les œuvres.

Le concept de réalisme ici proposé vise à la «nature» de l'architecture comme la somme de ses possibilités immanentes, en partie déterminées par le métier. La nature ou l'essence d'une chose ne peut être reconnue qu'à travers le changement. Le lieu de ce changement est l'histoire: c'est là que la «nature» de l'architecture se révèle.

Comme les autres arts, l'architecture est liée à l'expérience immédiate, autrement elle ne serait pas différente par exemple de la science. Renoncer à sa propre réalité conceptuelle et sensuelle (ne serait-ce au nom d'un engagement social) signifierait priver notre sensualité d'une expérience fondamentale. Vis-à-vis des tendances qui veulent éliminer le plaisir de l'architecture, il faut donc revendiquer le droit à ce plaisir.

3

18   Leading article by Bruno Reichlin and Martin Steinmann in *archithese* 19 (1976), *Realismus in der Architektur*

most theoretically oriented of the Ticinese generation. While reflecting in the exhibition catalogue on their common concerns with history, territory, and autonomy, Steinmann used these notions to develop an original understanding of architectural realism, detached from all-too-literal interpretations of "reality":

> Architecture is not able to designate the real ... directly, but only indirectly, by repeating forms which draw their meaning from appropriate socialized experiences—connotations. Architecture is able to connote the real, but not denote it ... if we now propose the question of realism in architecture, we notice that we must return to architecture for the answer: there we find the confirmation that the meaning of architecture derives from its relationship to itself, its autoreflexivity.[80]

Steinmann's theoretical notion of realism, developing across the *Tendenzen* exhibition text and the *architese* editorial, laid bare the double bind of architectural autonomy. On the one hand, the critic acknowledged architecture's obligation to react "to the ruling powers and to the prevailing ideologies."[81] On the other, he declared the primacy of formal and typological operations in the production of architectural meaning. The exhibition therefore entailed a process of interpretation of the Ticinese built output that transposed the dilemma of autonomy from the realm of buildings to that of theory. Through its emancipation from the buildings it sought to justify, the exhibition's theoretical argument acquired an operative autonomy of its own.[82]

80 Steinmann, "Reality as History [1998]," 253.
81 Steinmann, "Reality as History [1976a]," 155.
82 See fn. 3 regarding Tafuri's term "operative criticism."

CRITICAL CONSTRUCTS AND THE MYTH OF THE TICINO

The writings of Kenneth Frampton have contributed, substantially if unintentionally, to the construction of what the German historian Frank Werner called "the nebulous concept of the Ticino School."[83] Ticinese architecture appealed to Frampton as an ethically motivated pushback against the corporate, speculative, and culturally anonymous suburban sprawl decimating Ticino's natural landscape. He in turn framed Ticinese architecture as a creative synthesis of vernacular and avant-garde models, forging connections to local history and culture while claiming a progressive outlook, unencumbered by populist nostalgia. Previously, the recent Ticinese production had been primarily defined through its debt to postwar Italian theory, namely its topics of realism, neo-rationalism, and autonomy. For Frampton, these notions represented viable alternatives to the generic Cartesian space of late capitalism promoted worldwide through international modernism.[84] In contrast to the latter's technocratic and corporate procedures, Ticinese architecture could be promoted as an example of "critical regionalism." Through the definition of a sense of place, architecture defied the undifferentiated march of global hegemonies. The benefits of this reading were mutual. While the Ticinese production shored up Frampton's theses of critical regionalism, his own weighty profile strengthened its outreach and contributed to its international standing.

Frampton's input into this myth formation began in 1978 with the *Oppositions* article "Mario Botta and the School of the Ticino" (fig. 19). Its departing premise was the paradoxical emergence of an innovative architectural approach in the context of a "frontier-culture" between Italy and the rest of Switzerland.[85] Like others before him—namely Steinmann,

83 Frank Werner, "Der nebulöse Begriff der 'Tessiner Schule' oder wie ein Mythos entsteht," in *Neue Tessiner Architektur: Perspektiven einer Utopie*, ed. Frank Werner and Sabine Schneider (Stuttgart: Deutsche Verlags-Anstalt, 1989), 9–85.

84 Kenneth Frampton, *Modern Architecture: A Critical History*, Fourth edition (London: Thames & Hudson, 2007), 294.

85 Frampton, "Mario Botta," 2–3.

Reichlin, and Huet—Frampton presented the Italian-Swiss architecture as the built embodiment of Italian *Tendenza*, which he defined by the same cornerstones of "relative" architectural autonomy, the cultural significance of the city, and the use of history as a design resource. And like other international critics with little training in Swiss nuance, Frampton underestimated the pluralism of Ticino architecture. It was more convenient to package and disseminate a nominal "School of the Ticino," understood as a unified theoretical construct rather than a centralized institution in the canton itself. This titular concept was positioned as a demonstration of "the cultural survival of the European city-state," preparing the ground for its subsequent placement in the critical regionalist arena.[86]

In a consequential departure from previous commentaries, the *Oppositions* article for the first time singled out Botta's "central and catalytic role" in this production. For Frampton, Botta's designs were at the same time "unique" and "typical."[87] The typical aspects were, implicitly, those stemming from the common background of Ticinese praxis, but explicitly they belonged to the referential field of Italian theory. None of these approaches had been formulated by Botta in isolation; indeed, Frampton reserved the greatest praise for the unrealized urban projects he had achieved in collaboration with Snozzi.[88] Nevertheless, the critic's focus on Botta as a representative figurehead was consequential. What distinguished Botta from his Ticinese contemporaries—most of whom had trained at ETH Zurich—was his time in Venice: his architecture training at the Istituto Universitario di Architettura in Venice (IUAV) and the forma-

86 Frampton, "Mario Botta," 3.
87 Frampton, "Mario Botta," 3.
88 The article refers to the following projects: the Dorigny masterplan for the Ecole Federal Polytechnique de Lausanne (1970) in collaboration with Tita Carloni, Flora Ruchat-Roncati, Aurelio Galfetti, and Luigi Snozzi; the competition for Centro Direzionale, Perugia (1971) in collaboration with Snozzi; and the competition for the Zurich railway station (1978) in collaboration with Snozzi and Martin Boesch. Cf. Frampton, "Mario Botta," 4.

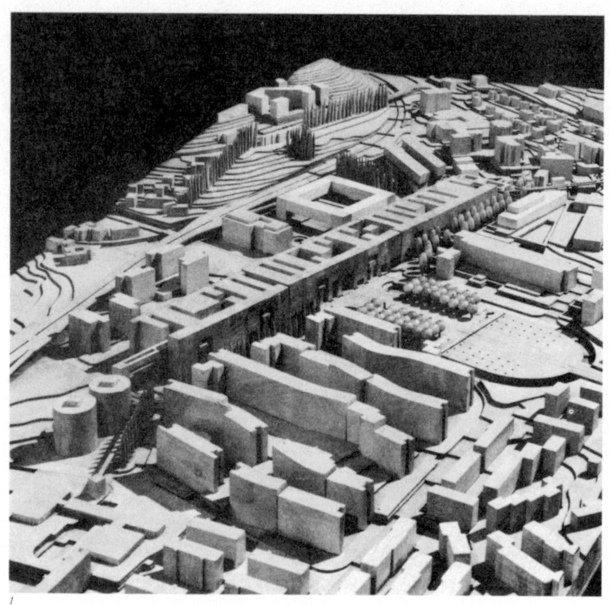

19 Frontispiece of Kenneth Frampton's article "Mario Botta and the School of the Ticino," *Oppositions* 14 (Fall 1978), showing the model of Mario Botta and Luigi Snozzi's collaborative competition entry for Centro Direzionale in Perugia, 1971

tive experiences of working for Carlo Scarpa and, briefly if intensely, with Le Corbusier and Louis Kahn on their late-career Venice projects. These individual markers highlighted Botta's personal narrative as distinct from the Ticinese protagonists—indeed, "unique" among them.

Frampton reprised his vision of a Botta-led regional school in a series of essays on critical regionalism throughout the 1980s.[89] These can be seen to fall into two categories: those where Ticinese and other regional architectures are subjected to full-fledged assessments as illustrations of critical regionalism; and the ones in which the theoretical framework predominates, expounded in points with nominal references to the regional architects.

The first category reworked the material initially included in the *Oppositions* article, namely in his 1983 *Perspecta* article "Prospects for a Critical Regionalism" and a new chapter in the second (1985) edition of *Modern Architecture,* entitled "Critical Regionalism: Modern Architecture and Cultural Identity."[90] Both texts astutely situated the Ticinese production within the Swiss political system, in the field of tension between "the cantonal system [that] serves to sustain local culture" and federal standards that enable "the penetration and assimilation of foreign ideas."[91] Frampton thus conceived of canton and federation as dialectically opposed terms, mirroring at a regional scale the conflict between culture and civilization in his construct of critical regionalism. In this sense, Ticinese architecture was acclaimed for "its capacity to condense the artistic potential

89 For a full-fledged pedigree of the notion of critical regionalism and the history of its adoption by Frampton, see Stylianos Giamarelos, "Authorial Agents," in *Resisting Postmodern Architecture: Critical Regionalism before Globalisation* (London: UCL Press, 2022), 89–121.

90 Kenneth Frampton, "Prospects for a Critical Regionalism," *Perspecta* 20 (1983): 147–162; Kenneth Frampton, "Critical Regionalism: Modern Architecture and Cultural Identity," chap. 5 in *Modern Architecture: A Critical History*, Fourth edition (London: Thames & Hudson, 2007), 314–27.

91 Frampton, "Prospects for a Critical Regionalism," 156.

of the region while reinterpreting cultural influences coming from the outside."[92]

That Frampton shored up his argument with Botta's work could be explained through the latter's design method of "building the site": a strategy of complementing land-scape formations with built forms (fig. 20).[93] Applicable to the geological (natural), as well as agricultural (man-made) characteristics of the region, this formulation would have strongly appealed to Frampton, for whom Ticino's dra-matic topography counteracted the "absolute *placelessness*" of technocratically flattened ground.[94] Botta's buildings thus shored up Frampton's notion of "bounded place-forms," rooted in the Heideggerian idea of boundary as an experi-ential rather than actual enclosure.[95] They qualified as such through spatial articulations that signaled different condi-tions of topography, use, and land ownership. Frampton described the houses as "bunker-belvederes," editing out un-desired views of speculative "placeless" suburbs and framing more salient aspects of the landscape.[96]

Conversely, the urban-scale projects in which Botta had collaborated with Luigi Snozzi and other Ticinese archi-tects were articulated as large civic figures, deploying the imagery of specific types (gallerias, viaducts) and materializ-ing "an indistinct urban boundary" without competing with the historical fabric.[97] However, the inner contradiction that arose from the buildings' anchorage into the existing land- or cityscapes, while creating strong topographical figures, was not addressed. Their ambivalence as both "bounded" and "primary" forms was subsumed under their capacity to

92 Frampton, "Prospects for a Critical Regionalism," 156.
93 Botta, "Academic High School."
94 Kenneth Frampton, "Towards a Critical Regionalism: Six Points for an Architecture of Resistance," in *The Anti-Aesthetic: Essays on Postmodern Culture*, ed. Hal Foster (Port Townsend, WA: Bay Press, 1983), 16–30, here 26.
95 Frampton, "Towards a Critical Regionalism," 25.
96 Frampton, "Prospects for a Critical Regionalism," 157.
97 Frampton, "Prospects for a Critical Regionalism," 157.

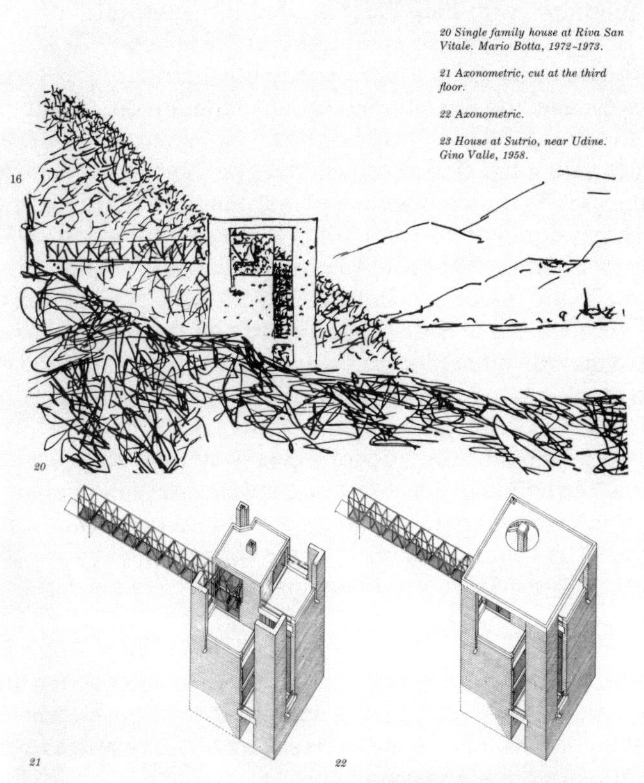

20 Mario Botta sketch and axonometric views of Casa Bianchi in Riva San Vitale (1972–73) as shown in Kenneth Frampton's article "Mario Botta and the School of the Ticino," *Oppositions* 14 (Fall 1978), p. 16.

"harmonize" with their location through interpretations of local types and "analogical" forms and finishes.[98]

The second and more speculative category of texts that focused on the demonstration of theoretical positions is illustrated by two essays written in 1983 and 1987, in which Frampton elaborated upon his definition of critical regionalism as an "architecture of resistance."[99] Botta's name featured again at the forefront of Ticinese production, as in the formulation "the recent Ticinese school of Mario Botta *et al.*"[100] In "Towards a Critical Regionalism: Six Points for an Architecture of Resistance," Botta's strategy of "building the site" was presented as an exemplary design method in the section "Culture versus Nature,"[101] whereas four years later, in "Ten Points on an Architecture of Regionalism: A Provisional Polemic," the "recent Ticinese school" was placed under the heading "The Myth and the Reality of the Region," in which Frampton acknowledged the ideas of "school" and "region" as cultural and institutional constructs—"necessary myths, as any self-consciously created culture must be."[102] This deliberateness points for the first time towards an instrumentalization of the ethical concept of resistance, which in the first essay was a primarily political proposition. Given the production's ultimate dependency on capitalist development, in Botta's case the question of resistance was reduced to an aesthetic stance, editing out spoiled views to emphasize the coming together of building and picturesque landscape.

Ticinese production did not subscribe equally to all points of Frampton's critical regionalism. To be sure, in its "recuperative, self-conscious, critical endeavor" it proved highly capable of adapting the historical forms of the local vernac-

98 Frampton, "Prospects for a Critical Regionalism," 157.
99 Frampton, "Towards a Critical Regionalism"; and Kenneth Frampton, "Ten Points on an Architecture of Regionalism: A Provisional Polemic," in *Architectural Regionalism: Collected Writings on Place, Identity, Modernity, and Tradition*, ed. Vincent Canizaro (New York: Princeton Architectural Press, 2006), 375–85.
100 Frampton, "Ten Points," 380.
101 Frampton, "Towards a Critical Regionalism," 26.
102 Frampton, "Ten Points," 380.

ular and creating a current dialogue with the past.[103] At the same time, the architecture was nothing if not visual. For this generation enthralled by Le Corbusier, smooth concrete became the default building material, clearly distinguishable from the pervasive vernacular materiality of rough masonry and render. Those projects using brick or stone emphasized hard surfaces and sharp contours, eliminating, alongside handicraft traces and traditional materials and techniques, any inherent nostalgia. And yet, despite its aversion to "nostalgic historicism," the Ticinese production's emphasis on the visuality aspects tended towards "scenography" rather than the tactility and tectonic coherence associated with critical regionalism.[104]

Frampton's reading of Ticinese production within the tension between regional "culture" and universalizing "civilization" mirrored the relation between local conditions and external readings. His use of the Ticinese output to illustrate critical regionalism significantly helped raise its profile worldwide, but only at the cost of detaching it from the context that had nurtured and shaped it. By fusing the incompatible personal approaches of Ticinese architects into one theoretical construct, and furthermore by subordinating their collective significance under one dominating personality, Frampton's readings overstepped into the domain of operative criticism.

As already mentioned, a consequence of Frampton's ratification was that Botta's professional "currency" increased considerably, projecting him into the realm of international stardom. Set apart from his Ticinese colleagues, Botta distanced himself from the collective narrative and, at the same time, from the common conditions encountered by all architects in Ticino. It is telling that the catalogue of his personal retrospective at the Museum of Modern Art in New York from late 1986 to early 1987 (the only Ticinese to be thus celebrated) mentioned neither his colleagues

103 Frampton, "Ten Points," 378.
104 Frampton, "Towards a Critical Regionalism," 19–20.

in the *Tendenzen* exhibition twelve years earlier nor the common regional context of their work.[105] Instead, the introductory essay by Stuart Wrede formulated a heroic personal narrative that positioned Botta directly in the global modernist lineage of Le Corbusier, Scarpa, and Kahn. Ticino, the actively formative background to Botta's work, was demoted to a passive topography for individual experimentation. This trajectory, from the collective to the individual and from the specific to the general, actively contradicted Frampton's thesis of critical regionalism. As Jorge Otero-Pailos later observed, the construct had been too subtle to escape misappropriation. Botta belonged to those critical regionalists who were "invited back from the repressed margin into the center of architectural discourse, at the price of exacting from them the language of the center."[106] From Maastricht to Tokyo and San Francisco to Seoul, his subsequent architecture became itself an agent of the "placelessness" Frampton had lamented.[107]

Listing critical regionalism's many refutations and revisions is not the aim here, but it is nonetheless worth revisiting Keith Eggener's insistence that as a top-down theoretical reading reinforced by authority figures, critical regionalism is itself "a postcolonialist concept."[108] Eggener argued that critical examinations of regional identity should include an analysis of their underlining political and ideological agendas[109]—work that, in Botta's case, has yet to be undertaken. Furthermore, for Alan Colquhoun, critical regionalism was itself an anachronism. If local specificity had once been the

105 Stuart Wrede, *Mario Botta* (New York: Museum of Modern Art, 1986), 8–21.

106 Jorge Otero-Pailos, "Surplus Experience: Kenneth Frampton and the Subterfuges of Bourgeois Taste," in *Architecture's Historical Turn: Phenomenology and the Rise of the Postmodern* (Minneapolis: University of Minnesota Press, 2010), 183–250, here 248-9.

107 Frampton, "Towards a Critical Regionalism," 26.

108 Keith L. Eggener, "Placing Resistance: A Critique of Critical Regionalism," *Journal of Architectural Education* 55, no. 4 (2002): 228–37, here 234.

109 Eggener, "Placing Resistance," 231.

preserve of autonomous, closed-off cultural regions, nowadays differences occurred in an unpredictable fashion within current formations of "large, uniform, highly centralised cultural / political entities."[110] Difference, Colquhoun contended, had become a matter of individual preference. It was "the result of the choices of individual architects who are operating from within multiple codes," themselves "the product of modern rationalization and the division of labour."[111]

While Eggener's and Colquhoun's readings might lay the ground for a more nuanced criticism of Ticino architecture, Frampton's programmatic theoretical projection had nevertheless far-reaching consequences, both in theory and practice. Botta's privileged position on Frampton's critical regionalist agenda led to an international standing not granted to any of his Ticinese contemporaries. His enhanced status at home and among non-architects lent sufficient leverage for Botta's most genuinely political project: the founding (together with, among others, Aurelio Galfetti) of the Accademia di Architettura in 1997. Affiliated to the Università della Svizzera italiana and located in Mendrisio, Botta's modest hometown, the Accademia explicitly adopted a humanistic position to complement the two federal polytechnics in Zurich and Lausanne. Over several years, Botta was instrumental in the academic appointments of several well-known architects and critics, including Frampton between 1998 and 2002. Thus, twenty years after coining a fictional "School of the Ticino," Frampton not only indirectly contributed to its actual creation but also directly to its curriculum. His lectures continued the exchanges between the US and Swiss academia and resulted in several new publications, including two focused on Ticino and Swiss

110 Alan Colquhoun, "Regionalism 1," in *Collected Essays in Architectural Criticism* (London: Black Dog, 2009), 280–286, here 285. Originally published in *Postcolonial Spaces*, 1992.
111 Colquhoun, "Regionalism 1," 284.

modernism.[112] Through the medium of critique, Frampton's early pronouncements morphed into self-fulfilling prophecy.

112 See for example the book of Frampton's own lectures at the Accademia di Architettura: Kenneth Frampton, *L'altro Movimento Moderno*, ed. Ludovica Molo, trans. Maddalena Ferrara (Mendrisio: Mendrisio Academy Press, 2015).

INTERMEZZO: THE ALPS AS CULTURAL BOUNDARY

The circulation of ideas follows its own course, and yet, like any current, is influenced by actual topographies. The Alpine passes to and from Ticino have regularly mediated theoretical and professional exchanges between Italian, Italian-Swiss, and German-Swiss architectural cultures. Separating a nominal north and south, the physical barrier of the Swiss Alps has given physical dimensions to a cultural distance. The architectural transfers during the 1960s and 1970s can thus be reframed as a species of crossings, in which the imagery of the Alps has played an active role.

In *The Architecture of the City* (1966), Aldo Rossi chose a popular nineteenth-century engraving of the Ponte del Diavolo, a dramatic infrastructure on the St. Gotthard Pass, to illustrate the confrontation between "nature and man's construction"[113] (fig. 21). Rossi argued for a conceptual understanding of the city as extending beyond its physical confines, and urbanity as the manifestation of civilization in the territory. To that effect, he examined "not only the visible image of the city and the sum of its different architectures, but architecture as construction," as urban artifacts set into specific relationships with their locality.[114] In a similar vein, art historian Albert Kirchengast later described the Gotthard as a "dialectical landscape," in which the (fictional) image of "pure" nature is permanently confronted with the actuality of human control.[115]

Alpine crossings were part of Rossi's commute between Milan and Zurich during his visiting professorship at ETH Zurich between 1972 and 1974, regularly by car in the company of his teaching assistants Bruno Reichlin and Fabio Reinhart.[116] The contemporary note in his diary, "anch'io

113 Aldo Rossi, *The Architecture of the City*, trans. Diane Ghirado and Joan Ockman (Cambridge, MA: MIT Press, 1982), 20. The print is *Vue du nouveau Pont du Diable sur la nouvelle route du St Gothard*, after Rudolph Dikenmann, ca. 1840–1851.

114 Rossi, *The Architecture of the City*, 21 and 23.

115 Albert Kirchengast, "Der Gotthard als dialektische Landschaft," in *Der Gotthard / Il Gottardo: Landscapes—Myths—Technology*, ed. Marianne Burkhalter and Christian Sumi (Zurich: Scheidegger & Spiess, 2016), 151–61.

116 Aldo Rossi, "An Analogical Architecture," in *Theorizing a New Agenda*

21　Rudolf Dikenmann,_Vue du nouveau Pont du Diable sur la nouvelle route de St. Gothard (View of the new Devil's Bridge on the new St. Gotthard route), ca. 1840–1851. The engraving, depicting a dialectical interplay between the natural and the human-made, was reproduced in Aldo Rossi's The Architecture of the City.

come Gastarbeiter" ("I, too, as a foreign worker") illustrates an attitude of political solidarity, if not a left-wing intellectual's romanticized identification with the generations of Italians traveling for work to Switzerland.[117] The mountain crossings mediated a range of personal and cultural experiences that subconsciously took shape in Rossi's architecture.[118] In his 1978 lecture at ETH Zurich, entitled "An Analogical Architecture," Rossi acknowledged his personal experience of the infrastructural galleries on this route, internalized during years of regular crossings and reemerging in his design for the galleries of the Gallaratese housing block on the outskirts of Milan:

> an aspect of this design ... made clear to me by Fabio Reinhart driving through the San Bernardino Pass, as we often did, in order to reach Zurich from the Ticino Valley; Reinhart *noticed* the repetitive element in the system of open-sided tunnels, and therefore the inherent pattern. I understood ... how I must have been conscious of that particular structure—and not only of the forms—of the gallery, of covered passage, without necessarily intending to express it in a work of architecture.[119]

The impact of Rossi's fragmented Swiss experiences is also apparent in his *Scientific Autobiography,* in which he repeatedly brings up Zurich's places and buildings, acquaintances

for Architecture: An Anthology of Architectural Theory, 1965–1995, ed. Kate Nesbitt (New York: Princeton Architectural Press, 1996), 345–53. Originally published in *Architecture and Urbanism* 56 (May 1976): 74–76, translated by David Stewart. For the significance of Rossi's Zurich teaching in a wider context, see Kurt W. Forster, "Architektur vor dem Verstummen retten," in *Aldo Rossi und die Schweiz: Architektonische Wechselwirkungen*, ed. Ákos Moravánszky and Judith Hopfengärtner (Zurich: gta Verlag, 2011), 119–130.

117 Aldo Rossi, *I quaderni azzuri*, ed. Francesco Dal Co (Milan: Electa; Los Angeles: Getty Foundation, 1999), notebook 11, February 28–June 6, 1972.

118 See Adrià Carbonell and Roi Salgueiro Barrio, "Notes on Aldo Rossi's Geography and History; the Human Creation," *Cartha* 2, no. 18 (2016): 36–37.

119 Rossi, "An Analogical Architecture," 350.

and colleagues from ETH Zurich, lectures attended and given there, and affinities with Germanic culture.[120] The wider pattern emerging here is the ripple effect of professional exchanges negotiated across the Alps.

Unsurprisingly, the Alps provide a significant background in the collage *La Città analoga,* assembled by Rossi with Reinhart, Reichlin, and their colleague Eraldo Consolascio for the 1976 Venice Biennale (fig. 22).[121] A reconstruction of the original sources used in the collage assigns the cartographic representation of mountains on the bottom left to the first edition of the Dufour Map (1845–1865), Switzerland's first federal survey.[122] A cornerstone in the construction of the country's national identity once described by Marc Angélil and Cary Siress as "saturated with ideology," the Dufour Map points to the power relations inscribed within the seemingly objective record of Swiss territory.[123] In the *Città analoga* collage, it is juxtaposed with the drawing of a winding road, a coda for mountain crossings similar to the Tremola Pass on the Gotthard but in fact collated from Rossi's own project for a town hall in Scandicci (with Massimo Fortis and Massimo Scolari,

120 Aldo Rossi, *A Scientific Autobiography*, trans. Lawrence Venuti (Cambridge, MA: MIT Press, 1981). Rossi includes references to two of Karl Moser's public buildings in Zurich: the Lichthof of the University of Zurich and the Kunsthaus (pp. 8–9; ill. 14); the book also references Paul Hofer's lectures at ETH Zurich (pp. 43–44); a self-confessed "Germanophilia" and significant discussion with Heinrich Helfenstein (p. 46); Rossi's own lectures and later teaching with Paul Hofer in 1977 to 1978 (pp. 50–51); the Limmat river (p. 69); and his childhood fascination with a book of Swiss railways timetables (p. 80).

121 The panel was shown as part of the exhibition *Europa-America: Centro storico-suburbio.* See Léa-Catherine Szacka, *Aldo Rossi, Bruno Reichlin, Fabio Reinhart, Eraldo Consolascio, ETH Zurich, Zurich, Switzerland, 1976* (Princeton University School of Architecture, n.d.), https://archive.ph/kNN0w. For a comprehensive iconographic analysis of the *Città analoga* collage, see Carsten Ruhl, "Im Kopf des Architekten: Aldo Rossis La Città analoga," *Zeitschrift für Kunstgeschichte* 69, no. 1 (2006): 67–98.

122 Dario Rodighiero, *The Analogous City: The Map* (Lausanne: Editions Archizoom, 2015).

123 Marc Angélil and Cary Siress, "Operation Switzerland: How to Build a Clockwork Nation," in *Mirroring Effects: Tales of Territory* (Berlin: Ruby Press, 2019), 707–94, here 707.

1968).[124] Similarly overlaid in the bottom left corner are plan and elevation surveys of Ticinese rural settlements, drawn by Rossi's students at ETH Zurich.[125] Rossi's own reluctance to clarify the sources and personal meanings attached to the collage indicate their nature as indicative, analogous, and ultimately subjective ("autobiographical") references. For him, "the panel suggests in a fairly plastic way the image of the different meaning which distinct projects produce through a relatively arbitrary editing … while trying to express a dimension of surroundings and of the memory."[126]   He admits that the Ticinese and Northern Italian references are specific: "Clearly, this panel shows a number of aspects of … a memory circumscribed to a certain territory, or better, to a country—Northern Lombardy, Lake Maggiore, and the Canton Ticino—with its signs and emblems."[127] By giving cultural unity precedence over the administrative and geo-political redistribution of territory, Rossi disregards the Swiss Italian frontier. The composition signals that the true border is the mountain—the geographical distance between different cultures that allows them to coexist without blending into each other.

The intellectual traffic between Italy and Switzerland moved both ways. In the course of his Zurich teaching, Rossi oversaw the production of several urban studies, most famously the so-called Rossi Plan of Zurich's historical center in 1973 to 1974, but also, in collaboration with Bernhard Hoesli and Paul Hofer, the Solothurn studies of 1977 to 1978.[128]

124 Rodighiero, *The Analogous City*.

125 See Giovanni Buzzi, "Costruzione del territorio e spazio urbano nel cantone Ticino: Rossis Beitrag zur Untersuchung der Kulturlandschaft," in *Aldo Rossi und die Schweiz: Architektonische Wechselwirkungen*, ed. Ákos Moravánszky and Judith Hopfengärtner (Zurich: gta Verlag, 2011), 97–106.

126 Aldo Rossi, "La città analoga: Tavola," *Lotus* 13 (December 1976): 5–8, here 7.

127 Rossi, "La città analoga," 6.

128 Aldo Rossi, S. Cantoni, and ETH Zurich Department of Architecture, *Zurigo: Kartenmaterial. Rilievo 1:1000 del piano terreno entro il perimetro delle mura barocche anno 1973* (Zurich: ETH Zurich, 1980), simply known as the "Rossi plan." For its conceptual and methodological bases see Ákos Moravánszky, "Formen

22 Aldo Rossi, Fabio Reinhart, Bruno Reichlin, and Eraldo Consolascio, *Città analoga*, collage, 1976 (detail, bottom left section of the collage). It shows references to the Alpine pass and to Ticino as a shared cultural basin.

According to Rossi's conceptual understanding of the city, the method was extended to the typological analysis of the Ticino territory, undertaken over five years with the engagement of students from ETH Zurich, some of whom were Ticinese. The result was *La costruzione del territorio*, an eight-hundred-page opus systematizing preindustrial vernacular settlements across the canton, which Rossi coedited with former collaborators Eraldo Consolascio and Max Bosshard (fig. 23).[129] Given Ticino's lack of metropolitan structures, they argued, its urbanity resided in settlement patterns formed by villages in the landscape, which forged a distinct relation between society and territory. This study comprised the systematic investigation of traditional residential typologies in rural Ticinese settlements in a manner closely associated with traditional ethnography.

The volume's cover featured a small reproduction of the previously mentioned *Città analoga* collage for the 1976 Venice Biennale, a deliberate reflection on the ever-shifting relation between urban form and collective memory. The *Città analoga* collage included precise cartographic references to Ticino as a cultural rather than political entity: part of Lombardy, bound by the territory's natural and built features alike.[130] With this, the Italian and Swiss collaborators acknowledged that formal and cultural appropriations were, to some extent, inevitable. By examining local vernacular motifs, Rossi and his Ticinese colleagues indicated a possible way for the regional architecture to create its own referential language, rooted in specific formal and typological motifs with local intelligibility (fig. 24).

exaltierter Kälte: Rossis Rationalismus und die Deutschschweizer Architektur," in *Aldo Rossi und die Schweiz: Architektonische Wechselwirkungen*, ed. Ákos Moravánszky and Judith Hopfengärtner (Zurich: gta Verlag, 2011), 209–222, especially pp. 215–217.

129　Aldo Rossi, Eraldo Consolascio, and Max Bosshard, *La costruzione del territorio: Uno studio sul canton Ticino* (Lugano: Fondazione Ticino Nostro, 1979).

130　See Aldo Rossi, "La Città Analoga: Tavola," in *Lotus* 13 (December 1976), 5–8; Dario Rodighiero et al., *The Analogous City: The Map* (Lausanne: Editions Archizoom, 2015).

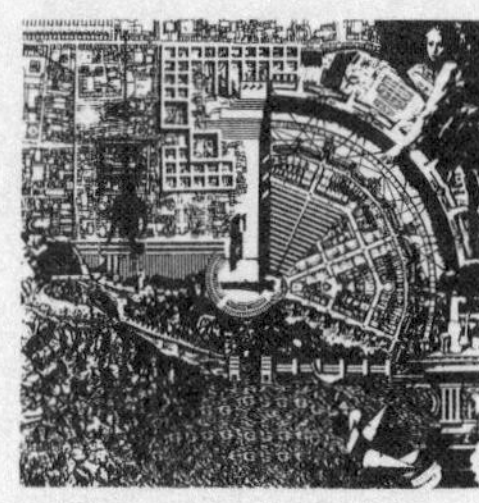

23 Cover of *La costruzione del territorio: Uno studio sul Canton Ticino*, 1979, by
Aldo Rossi, Eraldo Consolascio, and Max Bosshard, with the *Città analoga*
collage in medallion

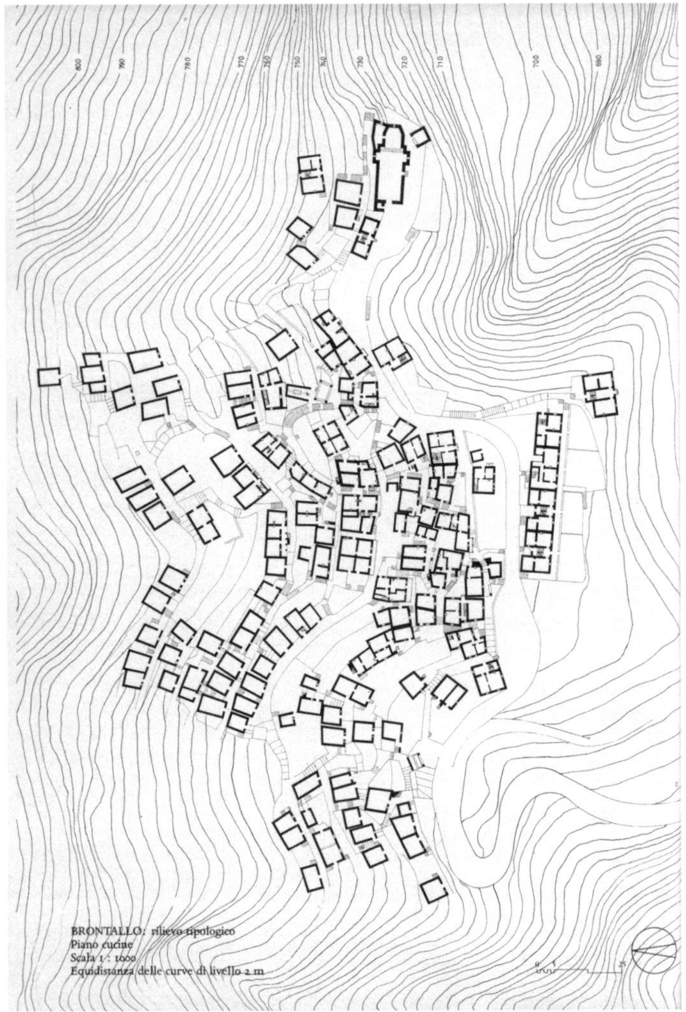

24 Typological survey of the village of Brontallo, Ticino. In Aldo Rossi, Eraldo
Consolascio, and Max Bosshard, *La costruzione del territorio*, 1979, p. 260.

For Reichlin and Reinhart, as for other Ticinese architects trained at ETH Zurich, the transalpine commute to Zurich was routine. The intellectual traffic in the postwar decades partly reversed Ticino's older historical and cultural connections with Italy. Since the Middle Ages, Ticinese architects and masons, Francesco Borromini included, had naturally gravitated towards the artistic centres of Italy (Rossi affectionately nicknamed his two assistants the "Borrominis of *Tendenza*"[131]). This profound connection was also perceptible during the early twentieth century as Italian rationalism penetrated Ticinese architecture circles. This situation was later reversed by a mix of economic, political, and administrative circumstances. The closure of the Italian border before and during World War Two reoriented the Ticinese towards their colleagues to the north, thus reinforcing the illusion of a Swiss cultural homogeneity.[132] As Reichlin and Reinhart's colleagues and contemporaries Paolo Fumagalli and Flora Ruchat-Roncati would later contend:

> the history of Swiss architecture between the two wars is exaggerated ... the extremely unified picture it presents is due to the fact that, in that period, the hegemonic culture is the Swiss-German one, and it positively conditions the whole country. It is involved in the international debate, it is open towards the north, it is the active reflection of the ideas and culture of central Europe. Its cultural superiority finds its institutional symbol in the Polytechnic of Zurich, the school in which all the Swiss who wanted to become architects or

131 Marcel Meili, Bruno Reichlin, and Fabio Reinhart, "Viele Mythen, ein Maestro: Kommentare zur Zürcher Lehrtätigkeit von Aldo Rossi, Teil II," *Werk, Bauen + Wohnen* 85, nos. 1/2 (1998): 37–44, here 39.

132 See Paolo Fumagalli, *Die Architektur der fünfziger und sechziger Jahre im Tessin zwischen Deutschschweiz und Norditalien*, ed. Anna Meseure, Martin Tschanz, and Wilfried Wang, vol. 5 (Munich: Prestel, 1998).

engineers had to study, whether they were German-speakers, French-speakers or Italian-speakers.[133]

As connection settled into custom, professional dialogues between Ticino and northern Switzerland strengthened after the Second World War. Ticinese critic Paolo Fumagalli, also an ETH Zurich graduate, argued that the training and teaching of Ticinese architects at ETH Zurich had imported to the south a professional culture based on lasting and good-quality construction, together with a new orientation towards the works of Le Corbusier, Frank Lloyd Wright, and Alvar Aalto.[134] And yet, as viewed from the south, the modernist culture at ETH Zurich in the 1950s and early 1960s was perceived as too technical and too dry for a well-rounded architectural education. The language barrier remained palpable for many Ticinese students, who tended to cluster to the Italian-Swiss professors, particularly Rino Tami. In turn, the connections made in Zurich continued in practice back in Ticino. Two-thirds of the twenty-one Ticinese practitioners featured in the exhibition *Tendenzen: Neuere Architektur in Tessin* were ETH graduates.[135] As we have seen, many of them later grouped together in social and professional networks, temporary collaborations, and long-term partnerships.[136]

Conversely, the appeal of the recent Ticinese production was due to its synthesis of modernist references, partly inherited from the authors' ETH training, partly learned from the Italian *Tendenza*. This synthesis did not fully obliterate the cultural distance embodied by the Alpine topography, but rather instrumentalized it. The Alps were primarily con-

133 Paolo Fumagalli and Flora Ruchat-Roncati, "L'unità e la diversità," *Parametro* 140, no. 7 (October 1985): 8.

134 Fumagalli, *Architektur der fünfziger und sechziger Jahre*, 93.

135 Mario Botta had studied at the IUAV in Venice. Of the remaining six architects trained through the apprenticeship route at the Lugano technical college, four were working in partnership with graduates of ETH Zurich.

136 See the example of Flora Ruchat-Roncati in Irina Davidovici and Katrin Albrecht, "Konzept Convivium," *Werk, Bauen + Wohnen* 104, no. 12 (2017): 8–19.

sumed as a seductive frame for the architecture, a marker of its (relative) remoteness, at most a transitional space for those visitors approaching Ticino's architectural sites from the north. And come they did, attracted by the buildings' intense coverage in professional publications, architecture guides, and anthologies.

LITERATURES OF A THIRD KIND

The juxtaposition of critical regionalist and emergent post-modernist theories in the late 1970s and early 1980s was accompanied by a growing yet markedly less critical interest in Ticinese architecture. On the footsteps of the probing secondary literature of the mid- and late 1970s, its historiography was enriched by sources of a third kind. This new gaze was less concerned with analyzing, qualifying, or intellectualizing the built production in Ticino. Mostly, it provided updates on the local auteurs, capitalizing on the international interest their work continued to arouse.

Of this fast-expanding volume of publications, many adopted the format of architectural monographs, with one or two introductory essays followed by taxonomies of built projects. A typical example of this proliferating literature is the 1983 catalogue *50 Anni di architettura in Ticino*, edited by Peter Disch.[137] Following an introductory essay by Tita Carloni, the book was an illustrated chronology of projects over three periods: 1930–40, 1940–60, and 1960–80, tracing parallels between the Ticinese buildings and contemporaneous international developments. The 1996 sequel *Architettura recente nel Ticino: 1980–1995* followed a similar format, bringing the survey to the present with added commentaries by Jacques Lucan and Paolo Fumagalli.[138] Disch, a local architect and coeditor (with Fumagalli) of the professional journal *Rivista tecnica*, was also behind several anthologies of Ticinese and later German-Swiss architecture.[139] The monographic format of his later publications—on the work of Mario Botta (1990), Livio Vacchini

137 Peter Disch, ed., *50 anni di architettura in Ticino, 1930–1980: Quaderno della rivista tecnica della Svizzera italiana* (Bellinzona: Grassico Pubblicità, 1983).

138 Peter Disch, Jacques Lucan, and Paolo Fumagalli, *Architettura recente nel Ticino, 1980–1995 / Neuere Architektur im Tessin, 1980–1995: Con un riassunto degli anni 1930–1980 / Mit einer Zusammenfassung der Jahre 1930–1980* (Lugano: ADV, 1996).

139 See, for instance, Peter Disch, ed., *Architektur in der deutschen Schweiz, 1980–1990: Ein Katalog und Architekturführer / L'architecture récente en Suisse alémanique / L'architettura recente nella Svizzera Tedesca*, Second edition (Lugano: ADV, 1991).

(1994), and Luigi Snozzi (1994 and 2004)—indicates how a rising interest in iconic figures supplanted the originally regional index of the works.

But the 1980s also brought, with the benefit of distance, more penetrating contributions to the Ticinese historiography. One was German architectural historian Frank Werner's 1980 *Bauwelt* article "Lieder, die man nicht erwartet" (Songs one does not expect), which sought to refute three common misconceptions: "that there is such thing as a 'Ticino School,' that Ticino architects build 'traditionally,' and that this architecture is 'elitist.'"[140] The agenda contained a fourth, implied, point: Werner's analysis of 1970s Ticinese projects led to the conclusion they were not, in any sense, postmodernist. Six years later, in another later *Bauwelt* report entitled "Ein Mythos auf dem Prüfstand" (A Myth on Trial), Werner criticized their association with postmodernism, alongside other "utopian myths" propagated in the international coverage of Ticinese architecture.[141] This stance was later reprised in the publication *Neue Tessiner Architektur: Perspektiven einer Utopie* (1989), coauthored with Sabine Schneider, which set out to separate fact from hagiographic coverage.[142] In this it proceeded systematically, subjecting the "nebulous concept" of Ticinese architecture to a neat historical periodization.[143]

Werner located the myth's origins in a cultural, historically preestablished condition: Ticino's consumption through the gaze of outsiders. The "exotic" appeal of its artistic avant-garde colonies, the "authentic" charm of its vernacular, and the fictional arcadia of "untouched" valleys, all located conveniently close to the cross-European motorway, had all contributed to the formation of a Ticino myth of which the

140 Frank Werner, "Lieder, die man nicht erwartet: Neue Architektur im Tessin," *Bauwelt* 39 (1980): 1720–38, here 1720.

141 Frank Werner, "Ein Mythos auf dem Prüfstand: Tessiner Architektur, 1980–86," *Bauwelt* 41-42 (1986): 1581–1615.

142 Frank Werner and Sabine Schneider, *Neue Tessiner Architektur: Perspektiven einer Utopie* (Stuttgart: Deutsche Verlags-Anstalt, 1989).

143 Werner, "Der nebulöse Begriff."

recent architecture of the 1970s was only the latest, "heroic" stage. The evolution of this myth from around 1960 to 1975 largely coincided with the chronology of the *Tendenzen* exhibition, although it had continued to consolidate throughout the 1980s. Werner examined the extent of Botta's international following and his artistic trajectory as he developed the trademark cylindrical villa plan, a further formulation of architectural autonomy better poised to circulate globally than locally. Ultimately, however, Werner and Schneider's 1989 volume contributed to the myth it had set out to expose. By singling out separate figures within sections of the book dedicated to Botta, Galfetti, Ivano Gianola, and Livio Vacchini, the book only further helped consolidate the myth's constituent parts.

Such thoughtful contributions to the literature on Ticinese architecture were vastly outnumbered by uncritical ones. The architecture's over-exposure in international publications in the late 1970s and 1980s set a lasting trend in architectural and educational tourism. As long as students and practitioners flocked to the region, the self-assigned duty of most of these books was not to analyze, but merely to describe. In the 1980s and 1990s, Ticino became the cultural nexus of a re-centered type of "Grand Tour," reinforced by the trend among universities in the United States to set up research centers in Ticino, at a distance from the more traditional destinations of Rome and Florence. Two architecture schools established subsidiaries in small villages in the region: the Southern California Institute of Architecture (SCI-Arc) in Vico Morcote (1983–1991) and Virginia Tech in Riva (from 1991 onward).[144] In picturesque yet secluded locations of the Ticino, these paradoxical institutions acted as conduits of centrality, putting American students in contact with local and European masters.

144 SCI-Arc Vico Morcote offered semester courses for US students taught by Ticino architects including Snozzi and Gianola. In 1991, Virginia Tech founded the Steger Center for International Scholarship in Riva San Vitale. See Martin Wagner, "SCI-Arc, Vico Morcote," *Werk, Bauen + Wohnen* 82, no. 9 (1995): 36–40.

In this context, US academic Gerardo Brown-Manrique, professor of architecture at the University of Miami, wrote the first architectural *Ticino Guide* in 1989.[145] Originally written in English and translated in German one year later, *The Ticino Guide* almost exclusively focused on the Ticino architecture of the 1970s and 1980s. The research behind it had been prompted, in the author's words, "by a curiosity about why so much publicized work of such interesting nature came from Switzerland and Italy"—in passing conflating the Italian *Tendenza* with the projects of Ticino-born protagonists.[146] The criteria for selection began from formal similarities, the buildings being described as "platonic solids built of common materials ... often perforated so as to augment the discourse between the outside and the inside spaces."[147] Interestingly enough, the author finally deferred to Kenneth Frampton's *Oppositions* article to state three further common—and yet contradictory—characteristics: the projects' "relative autonomy" as researches on type, their use of historical reference in contemporaneous analogies, and their importance as "monuments in embodying and representing the continuity of public institutions over time."[148] Implicitly he revealed where the conceptual roots of the publication lay, yet without lingering on the vexing contradiction of autonomy versus referentiality.

Other travel itineraries, following or preceding this first official guide, tended to be more improvised. The influx of students and professionals interested in seeing the buildings on location was accompanied by a rogue production of booklets, leaflets, and photocopied readers of institutional

<hr>

145 Gerardo Brown-Manrique, *The Ticino Guide* (New York: Princeton Architectural Press, 1989); Gerardo Brown-Manrique, *Architekturführer Tessin und Lombardei: Die neuen Bauten*, trans. Cornelia Berg-Brandl (Stuttgart: Hatje, 1990).

146 Brown-Manrique, *The Ticino Guide*, 7. Brown-Manrique's research into contemporary Ticinese architecture began in 1982 while teaching at the Miami University European Center in Luxembourg and continued in 1986/1987 under the affiliation of visiting scholar (see p. 5 of the acknowledgments in *The Ticino Guide*).

147 Brown-Manrique, *The Ticino Guide*, 10.

148 Brown-Manrique, *The Ticino Guide*, 10; cf. Frampton, "Mario Botta."

study trips.[149] These belonged to a further subgenre that began to emerge at this time: an informal gray literature of collected reprints of older publications. Defined by modest production values, it demonstrated the popularization of the Ticino architecture as a form of consumption. As the built output grew into a recognizable brand, the new publications and the reuse of previous ones became the basis for its ever more widespread marketing. This phenomenon pointed to the consolidation of the "Ticino myth" through subjective, partial, and often superficial reviews of the actual architecture. It also indicated the new possibilities enabled by the spread of reprographic technologies, by then widely used both in offices and architecture schools.

It is in this context that a further category of more insightful publications on the recent Ticinese architecture originated not only from outside the region, but also from outside the discipline. An important contribution to the discourse, the 1985 monograph *Architektur des Aufbegehrens: Bauen im Tessin* (An architecture of revolt: building in Ticino) was the result of a collaboration between Swiss journalist Dieter Bachmann and photographer Gerardo Zanetti.[150] On the face of it, this publication belongs to the historiographic category of mid- to late 1980s overviews of Ticinese architecture that formulated and perpetrated its narratives admiringly rather than questioningly. And yet, it stood out in its attempt at a more situated and nuanced interpretation of the work. Bachmann's leading essay "Architektur als Verzweiflung?" (Architecture as despair?) situated the work

149 See, for example, Frank Werner, *Neuere Architektur im Tessin: Exkursionsbericht* (Winterthur: Technikum Winterthur, 1978); Manfred Bukowski and Roland Ostertag, *Tessin: Bergdörfer und neue Villen—Dokumentation einer Studiengruppe des Fachbereichs Architektur der Technischen Universität Braunschweig*, Third edition (Braunschweig: TU Braunschweig, 1979); Abteilung für Architektur, Technikum Winterthur Ingenieurschule, ed., *Neuere Architektur im Tessin: Exkursion Herbst 1982—Eine Dokumentation* (Winterthur: Technikum Winterthur Ingenieurschule, 1982); Ente ticinese per il turismo, ed., *Itinerari di architettura moderna in Ticino / Auf den Spuren der modernen Architektur im Tessin* (Bellinzona: Ente ticinese per il turismo, 1989).

150 Bachmann and Zanetti, *Architektur des Aufbegehrens*.

of these architects in its political, cultural, and ideological contexts, before bemoaning its consumption as a mainly formal proposition.[151] To trace its developments, he organized the no longer so "new" Ticinese architectural phenomenon according to a tri-generational "family tree" (fig. 25). The "grandfather" figures (Mario Chiattone, Giuseppe Franconi, and Bruno Bossi) were the early pioneers of Ticinese modernism, with the established postwar protagonists (Rino Tami, Alberto Camenzind, and Peppo Brivio) cast as "fathers." Things became more complicated with the four chronological categories of "sons" born between 1927 and 1955, including among others Flora Ruchat-Roncati, the only woman on the roster.[152] This generational approach helped distinguish between a strongly ideological, post-1968 pioneering phase, a consolidation period in the late 1970s, and a "Hellenistic" phase in the early 1980s that lacked much of the earlier work's originality and political impetus. The authors thus formulated a polemical narrative of Ticinese architecture as a form of resistance, born out of the "despair" about environmental pollution and historical limitations, afterwards destined to enter a more superficial phase of stylistic streamlining.

This was not Bachmann's last word on this matter. A year later, he co-edited an issue of the Zurich-based arts magazine *Du*, dedicated to Ticino's "master architects" ("*Tessiner Baumeister*") (fig. 26).[153] Here Bachmann returned to his earlier periodization, using the architects' ideological and political beliefs as basis for assessment. In his piece for the magazine, he likened the three phases of Ticinese architecture to a hierarchy of "founders, apprentices, and epigones."[154] He expressed admiration for the architecture of Luigi Snozzi and Tita Carloni for its social ambitions,

151 Bachmann and Zanetti, *Architektur des Aufbegehrens*, 10–47.
152 Bachmann and Zanetti, *Architektur des Aufbegehrens*, 41.
153 Wolfhart Draeger and Dieter Bachmann, eds., *Du: Die Zeitschrift für Kunst und Kultur* 546 (August 1986).
154 Bachmann, "Gründer, Schüler, Epigonen."

Ein solcher Stammbaum würde so aussehen:

Die Großväter	Mario Chiattone, 1891–1957 Eugenio und Agostino Cavadini, 1881–1962 resp. 1907 Augusto Guidini, 1895–1970 Bruno Bossi, 1901 Giuseppe Franconi, 1901–69 Giovanni Bernasconi, 1905	Die »Übervater« Giuseppe Terragni Le Corbusier Frank Lloyd Wright Walter Gropius Mies van der Rohe Otto Rudolf Salvisberg … und die »Asconeser Architekten«
Die Väter	**Rino Tami,** 1908 Alberto Camenzind, 1914 Franco Ponti, 1921 Peppo Brivio, 1923 Sergio Pagnamenta, 1923 Dolf Schnebli, 1928	Emil Fahrenkamp Max Schmucklerski Carl Weidemeyer
Die Söhne I	Bruno Brocchi, 1927 **Tita Carloni,** 1931 **Luigi Snozzi,** 1932 Livio Vacchini, 1933	
Die Söhne II	Peter Disch, 1933 Giancarlo Durisch, 1935 Mario Campi, 1936 Aurelio Galfetti, 1936 Flora Ruchat, 1937 Guido Tallone, 1939 **Mario Botta,** 1943	Die neuen Meister Richard Meier Venturi und Rauch Louis Kahn Aldo Rossi Oswald M. Ungers
Die Söhne III (68er …)	Paolo Fumagalli, 1941 Marco Krähenbühl, 1941 Bruno Reichlin, 1941 Fabio Reinhart, 1942	
Die Söhne IV	Bernegger, 1942, Keller, 1948 und Quaglia, 1944 Ivano Gianola, 1944 **Roni Roduner,** 1944 Rudy Hunziger, 1946 Paolo und Franco Moro, 1945 und 1948 **Elio Ostinelli,** 1948 Fosco Moretti, 1950 **Giovanni Gherra,** 1953 **Antonio Bassi,** 1955 **Dario Galimberti,** 1955	

25 Genealogy of Ticinese architecture ("grandfathers," "fathers," "sons," "masters"), in Dieter Bachmann and Gerado Zanetti, *Architektur des Aufbegehrens: Bauen im Tessin* (An architecture of revolt: Building in Ticino), Birkhäuser, Basel, 1985, p. 41. This generational self-understanding is comparable to that in the preparatory notes for the *Tendenzen* exhibition (see fig. 14).

suggesting that these two architects' explicit left-wing political affiliations had thwarted to some extent their professional careers.

All in all, since its launch in 1941, *Du* has dedicated at least six thematic issues to cultural aspects of the canton of Ticino, of which three were concerned primarily with architecture, considered collectively in 1986, and in the form of individual biographies in 1989 and 2021.[155] Given *Du*'s status as an established cultural institution in German-speaking Switzerland, its choice of topics is a reliable indicator of artistic currency. It is therefore notable that its coverage of Ticinese architecture moved from the consideration of a group production to a focus on individual protagonists. If *Tessiner Baumeister* addressed the most general aspects of the Ticinese architecture, the later issues focused on its best-known contemporary "masters": *Luigi Snozzi und das Politische in der Architektur* (Luigi Snozzi and the political in architecture) in 1989 and *Mario Botta und die Architektur des Sakralen* (Mario Botta and the architecture of the sacred) in 2021. Bachmann, together with Wolfhart Draeger, was behind the earlier two issues.

Tessiner Baumeister constitutes an informal epilogue to the heroic phase of the recent Ticinese architecture. But unlike most architectural anthologies on this work, it grounded the built production in its place and in its—often contradictory—history. The analyses proceeded in a dialectical manner, spanning from Borromini to Snozzi, from international exports to the local vernacular, from group awareness to individual personalities. Regarding the new generation, the issue mentioned Galfetti, Campi, Botta, Gianola, Vacchini, and Snozzi. The latter was singled out in a brief portrait, written by Diego Peverelli, as "the actual driver" of the Ticinese

---

155 Draeger and Bachmann, eds. (1986); Dieter Bachmann, ed., *Du: Die Zeitschrift der Kultur* 585 (November 1989); Oliver Prange, ed., *Du: Das Kulturmagazin* 906 (May 2021).

26 Cover of *Du* 546 (Aug. 1986), *Tessiner Baumeister*, edited by Wolfhart Draeger
and Dieter Bachmann, showing the elevator tower, part of Aurelio Galfetti's
refurbishment of Castelgrande in Bellinzona

production.[156] The accompanying interviews with his contemporaries were, despite their brevity, revealing.[157] Vacchini, when asked about the rapport with the canton's important architectural history, answered with characteristic directness: "Why does one hear so much about contemporary Ticinese architecture? Because we're good."[158] For him, the Ticino phenomenon had less to do with history or geography than with the coincidental emergence of a few interesting practitioners at the same time and place—presumably the reason that *Du* had curated the topic to begin with.

As the editor of *Du* between 1988 and 1998, Bachmann addressed the theme on two later occasions. The first was the monographic issue *Luigi Snozzi und das Politische in der Architektur*, which depicted Snozzi (in his own words) as a "Don Quixote," engaged in an idealistic battle with an imperfect reality.[159] The subtitle, *Der radikalste Tessiner Architekt* (The most radical Ticinese architect), suggested an interest in architecture's social and political potential above an intra-disciplinary interpretation of "radicalism" (fig. 27). Indeed, Bachmann's editorial alluded to Snozzi's political affiliation as the main reason for him having been refused a permanent position at ETH Zurich—a move otherwise described as "inexplicable" considering his profile as a prominent practitioner and charismatic teacher.[160]

The last issue of *Du* that deserves mention in terms of Bachmann's editorial tenure does not concern Ticinese architecture at all. The May 1992 issue, entitled *Pendenzen: Neuere Architektur in der deutschen Schweiz—Eine Standortbestimmung* (Pending issues: new architecture in German Switzerland—a positioning), focused on another

---

156 Diego Peverelli, "Porträt Luigi Snozzi," ed. Wolfhart Draeger and Dieter Bachmann, *Du: Die Zeitschrift für Kunst und Kultur* 546 (August 1986): 71.

157 Lina Kälin, "Vier Fragen an fünf Architekten," ed. Wolfhart Draeger and Dieter Bachmann, *Du: Die Zeitschrift für Kunst und Kultur* 546 (August 1986): 68–71.

158 Kälin, "Vier Fragen," 70.

159 Dieter Bachmann, ed., "Ein Partisan: Editorial," *Du: Die Zeitschrift der Kultur* 585 (November 1989): 11–17, here 15.

160 Bachmann, "Ein Partisan: Editorial," 11.

27 Cover of *Du* 585 (Nov. 1989), *Luigi Snozzi und das Politische in der Architektur*, edited by Dieter Bachmann. The editor's description of Snozzi as the "most radical Ticinese architect" highlighted his political orientation, conflating it with the aesthetic dimensions of the work.

architectural subculture, this time in northern Switzerland.[161] The title knowingly paraphrased that of Martin Steinmann's 1975 exhibition, substituting *Tendenzen* for the rhyming *Pendenzen* (meaning in German pending, open issues). The parallel alerted the magazine's cultured audience to the emergence of a new, this time German-Swiss, regional production of note. By referring to the ETH Zurich exhibition, the play of words acknowledged its special role in having repackaged a similarly regional architecture for a wider, international, audience. Moreover, it placed the German-Swiss architecture on the same (methodological) trajectory as the Ticinese *Tendenzen* and the Italian *Tendenza*, while at the same time pointing to its new and individual potential.

In this expanding 1980s literature on Ticinese architecture, a special place is occupied by Thomas Boga's bulky anthology *Tessiner Architekten: Bauten und Entwürfe, 1960–1985*.[162] Published in 1986, it represents in many ways the culmination of the reiterative, eminently gray, literature of office-compiled and home-made guides dedicated to the 1960s and 1970s Ticinese architecture (fig. 28). It also shares a lot with the initial *Tendenzen* catalogue, not least because Boga's involvement in the initial exhibition continued with organizing its subsequent re-installations in the intervening decade. *Tessiner Architekten* reformatted much of the exhibition's original material, alongside excerpts from many other publications on the topic, all in the form of photocopied facsimiles. It amounted, in substance, to an extensive, large-scale scrapbook of earlier sources. At almost four hundred pages and with some 2,500 illustrations covering three hundred projects since 1960, this book was no longer the advocate of a marginal regional avant-garde. Its oversizing, as much as its additive photocopied content, was suggestive of unrealistic growth. The greatest merit of

161 Dieter Bachmann, ed., *Du: Die Zeitschrift der Kultur* 615 (May 1992).

162 Thomas Boga, ed., *Tessiner Architekten: Bauten und Entwürfe, 1960–1985 / Ticino Architects, Buildings and Projects, 1960–1985 / Architetti Ticinesi, Edifici e progetti, 1960–1985* (Zurich: ETH Zurich, 1986).

Tessiner Architekten was inadvertent: by reproducing the most important information—buildings, architects, articles and reviews—of the Ticinese *Tendenzen*, it became its analogue database, a general record of its historiography to date. Boga's credentials, his role in the initial *Tendenzen* exhibition, and his continued affiliation with ETH Zurich served to lend gravitas to this no doubt lovingly compiled patchwork of earlier sources.

Backlash was swift. It came in the form of an editorial in *Werk, Bauen + Wohnen* entitled "Ticino Architects: Or Four Theses in Xerox Technology," written by Ticinese architect and critic Paolo Fumagalli.[163] In the German-Swiss arena of this established journal—with full French and English translations besides—Fumagalli delivered a short, powerful attack on the superficial reception of Ticinese architecture. This editorial was not intended as a book review, even though its author made his opinions clear. Having used indifferent systems of classifications that placed masters and epigones in a position of equivalence, Boga's anthology, he argued, propagated a distorted view of the architecture and its protagonists.

Understandably, however, Fumagalli primarily took issue with the book's manner of collecting and disseminating information by using facsimiles of previous publications—what he called the rise of the "xerographic book."[164] Fumagalli saw the excessive use of photocopy technology as symptomatic of the rise of an architectural plagiarism based on the superficial reproduction of forms. As the reproductions extended from books to buildings, the Ticinese architecture's formal vocabulary was widely adopted as a generic lingua franca, without the requisite understanding of either its origins or meanings. Thus, photocopying stood

163 Paolo Fumagalli, "Tessiner Architekten: Oder vier Thesen über die Xerox-Technologie / Les architectes tessinois: Ou quatre thèses sur la technologie Xérox / Ticino Architects: Or Four Theses in Xerox Technology," *Werk, Bauen + Wohnen* 73, no. 10 (1986): 2–3.

164 Fumagalli, "Tessiner Architekten," 3.

28 Cover of *Tessiner Architekten: Bauten und Entwürfe, 1960–1985* (1986), edited by Thomas Boga. The medallion features Mario Botta and Luigi Snozzi's collaborative competition entry for Centro Direzionale in Perugia, 1971.

for a more general flattening—of built architecture and historiography alike—into a set of professional data ripe for exploitation. For Fumagalli, these parallel developments amounted to material and intellectual theft. Both forms of dissemination capitalized on the architecture's critical currency without contributing anything new to the discourse: "This cultural (and material) robbery takes place within an area already looted to a great extent ... where the topic to be treated is so fashionable as to insure the immediate interest of readers / xerox enthusiasts."[165] The article voiced the frustration of Ticinese architects, caught between the restrictions of everyday practice and the wider fictionalization of their own experience. Meanwhile, the critic argued, contrived theoretical readings overlooked very real issues, such as the insensitive speculative building and the environmental damage perpetrated upon the Ticino landscape:

> And the Ticino itself? To be honest, we from the Ticino are quite fed up with it. We are tired of reading the same kind of fiction about *the Ticino School* for over ten years now. ... Actually battles are fought elsewhere (today as well as yesterday) and then about other topics, too. Not least to save the Ticino (the non-xeroxable that is) from ecological disaster as well as the equally dreadful one of jerrybuilding it has been threatened by for decades.[166]

This embittered lament saw the wider reception of Ticinese architecture as a form of cultural appropriation. Indeed, its (critical or uncritical) coverage indicates that the many ways in which it was probed, instrumentalized, justified, or intellectualized came mostly from the outside. This rendered the built works as passive objects of investigation. The literature of the 1980s was uneven in quality and scope, displaying varying levels of critical engagement and historical

---

165 Fumagalli, "Tessiner Architekten," 3.
166 Fumagalli, "Tessiner Architekten," 3.

awareness. It covered genuine attempts at understanding the architecture, along more cynical ones at capitalizing upon its appeal. Some English-language commentators sought to frame it as a potential source for postmodernism (the Swiss would have none of it) or critical regionalism (likewise met with skepticism).[167] Regardless of their different agendas, these publications commonly tended to focus on the same architects whose names already drew widespread recognition. This provided them with additional cultural capital as part of the star-architect system, while leaving others by the wayside.

Ranging from neutral collections of projects to polemical commentaries, this literature articulated a spectrum of positions across the dialectics of historicity and contemporaneity, international currency and vernacular authenticity, artistic individuality and collective endeavor. From modest photocopied leaflets to high-end, full-color monographs, these publications served a shared ulterior motive: the amassing of capital, both economic and cultural. The intentions of the authors, editors, and publishers were mostly projective, using Ticinese architecture as a vehicle for external readings, some of them more accurate than others. At its most problematic, this literature peddled fictions—inasmuch as neither artistic integrity nor political resistance can be articulated as pure and absolute positions, isolated from the everyday operations of architecture in its historically restricted conditions.

---

167 For the rejection of postmodernism in the contemporaneous Swiss discourse, see Davidovici, "Issues of Realism."

THE RESISTANCE OF THE LOCAL

How did the Ticinese react to the attention, at once intrusive and flattering, lavished upon their everyday operations? In that respect, Fumagalli's public reaction to the Ticino "fiction" propagated by "xerographic books" discussed in the previous chapter is somewhat of an exception.[168] For other local architects, the external reception of their projects might have seemed too distant or of too little consequence; possibly exploitative, but also potentially useful. Whatever the reasons, the Ticinese's default response was ambiguous silence.

Parallel to the external readings, the insights offered by the protagonists themselves are less visible. Local commentaries were largely written in Italian, occasionally in German or French, and almost never translated into English. Despite their more limited circulation, insider narratives could offer some of the most lucid readings of the recent Ticinese architecture in terms of its economic and cultural impact. Most often staying away from overly theoretical framings, they focused instead on the historical, political, and economic conditioning of the built production. The main commentators were politically engaged intellectuals, familiar with—and sometimes vocally critical of—the reality on the ground. Detached from the economy of architectural practice and criticism encountered in the international historiography, they enjoyed a freedom granted simultaneously by local know-how and wider anonymity. Through detailed and accurate readings of the political and territorial context of the architecture, their testimonies sought to resist the (mis)conceptions propagated globally as the "Ticino myth." Of relatively little interest to external critics until now, they provide a poignant dimension to the notion of Ticinese architecture as an architecture of resistance.

Fumagalli is foremost among these less-known insiders. Trained like many of his contemporaries at ETH Zurich, he combined his practice in Ticino with teaching and writing. Before taking up his editorial role with the prestigious (Swiss-

168 Fumagalli, "Tessiner Architekten."

German) professional journal *Werk, Bauen + Wohnen* in 1983, between 1972 and 1982 Fumagalli had coedited, together with Peter Disch, the fortnightly *Rivista tecnica della Svizzera Italiana* (the technical review of Italian Switzerland).[169] Under Fumagalli, *Rivista tecnica* became a consistent vehicle for the dissemination of local viewpoints, complementing a running commentary on the contemporary Ticinese architecture with updates on associated developments in regional politics and urban planning. Throughout Fumagalli's editorship, *Rivista tecnica* covered the regional contemporary architecture not as an exotic phenomenon but as an everyday matter steeped in Ticino's specificity (fig. 29). The first issue edited by Fumagalli and Disch in January 1972 was programmatically themed *Pianificazione urbana* (urban planning). It outlined a new agenda for the journal as a "chronicle of buildings in our canton, of how we design, think and plan, a chronicle, positive or negative, of interventions in our territory. And of arbitrary absences. A chronicle also of what could be done."[170]

Following on this intention, during his first year as editor Fumagalli organized the overview "5 anni di architettura ticinese" (5 years of Ticinese architecture). The resulting feature, published over two consecutive numbers in 1972/1973, covered thirty-two Ticinese buildings completed since the late 1960s.[171] While this could be seen as a dress rehearsal for the projects included in the *Tendenzen* exhibition in 1975, the selection did not have the same generational index, nor

169 *Rivista tecnica: Rivista indipendente di architettura pubblicata della Svizzera Italiana* was the joint publication of two cantonal professional associations: the Ticino section of the Swiss Society of Engineers and Architects (SIA) and the Associazione Ticinese di Economia delle Acque: Ordine Ticinese Ingegneri e Architetti (ATEA: OTIA). Following from the earlier *Rivista tecnica della Svizzera Italiana*, active between 1910 and 1964, it ran from 1965 to 2005.

170 Paolo Fumagalli and Peter Disch, "Questo numero [editorial]," *Rivista tecnica della Svizzera Italiana* 63, no. 2 (January 31, 1972): 38–39, here 38.

171 Paolo Fumagalli and Peter Disch, "5 anni di architettura ticinese," pt. 1, *Rivista tecnica della Svizzera Italiana* 63, no. 24 (December 31, 1972): 1222–1253; Paolo Fumagalli and Peter Disch, "5 anni di architettura ticinese," pt. 2, *Rivista tecnica della Svizzera Italiana* 64, no. 2 (January 31, 1973): 36–67.

29   The professional journal *Rivista tecnica* provided a nuanced commentary of Ticino's development of architecture and infrastructure. Shown here are covers of issue 2 (1973), *5 Anni di architettura ticinese*, the programmatic survey of regional architecture that marked the new editorship of Paolo Fumagalli and Peter Disch; issue 11 (1975) *Architettura per la scuola* featuring Mario Botta's Scuola Media in Morbio Inferiore of 1975; issue 3 (1976) *Abitazione e studio a Riva S. Vitale* featuring Giancarlo Durisch's house and atelier of 1975; and issue 3 (1977) *Architettura non construita* featuring Bruno Reichlin and Fabio Reinhart's project for a single-family house in Vezio of 1975.

were the architects and their buildings curated according to external agendas. In this instance, all registered architects in the canton were invited to nominate their own buildings. The editors explicitly encouraged the inclusion of "minor" works, acknowledging that the overview might lose "some of its bite, but none of its interest."[172] In comparison to the curated content of the *Tendenzen* exhibition a couple of years later, this strategy served to paint a more balanced and accurate picture.

Looking back, Fumagalli found that the declared critical intention of *Rivista tecnica* had given rise to a "certain complicity" among the local professional community, heightening its self-perception as a collective, however heterogeneous.[173] A number of shared concerns and sensibilities—with heritage, territory, and type—led to further polemics addressed to the local professional community, as well as regular retrospectives of its built production. The self-reflection on local issues did not occur in absolute isolation. *Rivista tecnica* also published extensive features on Hans Scharoun, British new towns, documenta 5 in Kassel, and other international projects. More typical of a regional periodical, it translated articles and debates that had an immediate relevance for the local audience into Italian, for example a debate on the current state of Ticinese architecture, initiated by the Swiss-German periodical *Werk* in 1972.[174] Notably, however, the built architecture was consistently viewed in the wider context of the region. For instance, a three-part review of the schools and kindergartens built in the Ticino between 1971 and 1975 began with the full reproduction of the text of the

172 Paolo Fumagalli and Peter Disch, "Questo numero [editorial]," *Rivista tecnica della Svizzera Italiana* 63, no. 24 (December 31, 1972): 1220.

173 Paolo Fumagalli, "Diario dell'architetto, 26 Novembre 2012: A Flora Ruchat," *Archi: rivista svizzera di architettura, ingegneria e urbanistica / Schweizerische Zeitschrift für Architektur, Ingenieurwesen und Stadtplanung* 6 (2012): 64–66.

174 Peverelli and Burckhardt, "Banca della Svizzera Italiana, Lugano."

educational reform that had made their construction necessary.[175]

The magazine took a stand politically, too, although left-wing sympathies were never openly declared. Speculative development, destructive planning, and environmentally dubious practices were called out in an investigative issue of *Rivista tecnica* entitled "Contraddizioni di un territorio in espansione" (Contradictions of an expanding territory), an editorial collaboration between Fumagalli, Flora Ruchat-Roncati, Ivano Gianola, and Giancarlo Durisch (fig. 30).[176] Instead of the usual architectural focus on buildings, this polemical number tackled traffic pollution in Lugano and the privatization of water resources in the Maggia valley, documenting the "manipulation of the environment by the ruling class."[177] Its use in public debates had concrete political repercussions: soon after, a referendum put a stop to municipal plans for a four-lane lakeshore motorway in Lugano.[178] It was a rare case of a professional debate overflowing in the public sphere. In the quality of their content, critical analysis, and graphic design standards, the 1970s volumes of *Rivista tecnica* hovered well above those of a typical periodical of restricted circulation.

The airing of local perspectives was not restricted to local publications; indeed, in external ones they could reverberate more widely. Such was the case with the inclusion of an extended interview with Ticino philosopher and art historian Virgilio Gilardoni (1916–1989) in Bachmann and Zanetti's *Architektur des Aufbegehrens*, discussed in the previous chapter.[179] Gilardoni's involvement was a strategic editorial choice. A committed communist and a

175 Redazione [Paolo Fumagalli and Peter Disch], "Architettura per la scuola (part 1)"; "Architettura per la scuola (part 2)"; "Architettura per la scuola (part 3)."

176 Fumagalli, Paolo, Flora Ruchat-Roncati, et al., "Contraddizioni di un territorio in espansione. Due esempi: Valle Maggia e Lugano," *Rivista tecnica della Svizzera Italiana* 64, no. 12 (June 30, 1973): 558–73.

177 Fumagalli, Ruchat-Roncati, et al., "Contraddizioni," 561.

178 Fumagalli, "Diario dell'architetto," 65.

179 Dieter Bachmann and Gerardo Zanetti, eds., "Die Moral und die Wirk-

30 Cover of *Rivista tecnica* no. 12 (June 1973), edited by Paolo Fumagalli and
Peter Disch with guest editors Flora Ruchat-Roncati, Giancarlo Durisch and
Ivano Gianola, featuring a dystopian image of the dry Maggia riverbed.
Raising, ahead of its time, the specter of environmental destruction, the issue
looked beyond the autonomous architecture objects and had a powerful
political impact at the cantonal level.

towering figure among the canton's left-wing intellectuals, he had long positioned himself as the archivist of Ticino's cultural patrimony. In 1960, Gilardoni had set up the journal *Archivio Storico Ticinese* (Ticinese historical archive) as an independent platform that he led until 1986, expanding its art-historical commentary to include a focus on culture and politics.[180] An established advocate of the local heritage, his vocal criticism of its neglect had sometimes put him on a collision course with the cantonal authorities.

With respect to architecture, Gilardoni's historical formation allowed him a different perspective than that of practitioners and architecture critics. This was already suggested by his authoritative contribution to *Architektur des Aufbegehrens*, entitled "Die Moral und die Wirklichkeit: Eine Zurechtsetzung" (Morality and reality: a rectification).[181] In this interview, the historian debunked the common misconceptions regarding the new Ticinese architecture by analyzing its political conditions and situating it within a layering of historical, economic, and cultural formations going back centuries. With an extensive historical appraisal of the Ticino context, Gilardoni identified culturally embedded tensions between political doubt and cultural energy, collectivism and tribalism, modernism and provincialism. Thus, the recent Ticinese architecture had to be understood within a wider context considering the tradition of traveling master builders, a vernacular based on precarious resources, the rise of a new way of life, often economically dependent on tourism, and the environmental destruction that had accompanied the construction of modern infrastructure.

In these conditions, the "good" architecture in the Ticino had flourished in the 1970s thanks to a short period of politi-

lichkeit: Ein Gespräch mit dem Historiker Virgilio Gilardoni," in *Architektur des Aufbegehrens: Bauen im Tessin* (Basel: Birkhäuser, 1985), 175–86.

180 See Fabio Dal Busco and Chiara Orelli, "Virgilio Gilardoni," in *Historisches Lexikon der Schweiz (HLS)*, https://hls-dhs-dss.ch/de/articles/010181/2007-09-06/.

181 Bachmann and Zanetti, "Die Moral und die Wirklichkeit."

cal, cultural, and economic progress during the late 1950s and early 1960s. At the time, two liberal politicians, Franco Zorzi and Plinio Cioccari, had sought to legally curb speculative construction. Although their political influence had been short lived, they nevertheless had opened a window of opportunity for progressive architects: Rino Tami was put in charge of the motorway infrastructure design, Tita Carloni had official responsibilities for the Swiss national exposition in Lausanne in 1964 and the restoration of the Bellinzona castles, and Luigi Snozzi was placed on the *Commissione cantonale delle bellezze naturali* from 1962 until 1974. In parallel to political developments were the cultural horizons of a new "university generation" of Ticinese architects, artists, writers, and professionals, whose access to higher education had developed a double perspective, as conditioned by the issues of European reconstruction as by local agendas for renewal.[182] Economically, too, conditions had been propitious. The influx of capital from the north and of southern "hot money," the development of the banking and local construction sectors, and the cantonal injection of 600 million francs into school construction had generated a construction bonanza of the 1960s and 1970s in which high-quality architecture remained nevertheless in minority. As Gilardoni pithily put it: "when everybody builds, there is place for a few good buildings."[183] The number of "avant-garde" projects in the regional production was not only proportionally insignificant, but directly benefited only a restricted, predominantly middle-class community of everyday users and homeowners. For Gilardoni, the misalignment of the recent Ticinese architecture's ideological fundaments and the historical context in which it operated opened a defining paradox. Despite the left-wing professional credential of many of the architects, they found themselves on a resolutely bourgeois trajectory, serving a professional middle-class focused on family and

182 Bachmann and Zanetti, "Die Moral und die Wirklichkeit," 183.
183 Bachmann and Zanetti, "Die Moral und die Wirklichkeit," 185.

individual life. This meant that the mass housing typologies and configurations they might have felt ideologically inclined to experiment with—as earlier modernist generations had—were no longer available to them:

> what is offered here is no solution for the collective, like for example the *Höfe* of Red Vienna. The working class for which these had been built exists no longer in that sense, neither do projects for such solutions. For this reason, the new Ticinese architecture is also not revolutionary. The merit of these architects was to find a solution for the family house that is neither bourgeois nor petit bourgeois.[184]

In this intricate context, Gilardoni concluded, the regional index of Ticinese architecture had been defined for, and by, an outside audience. In reality, "there is no new Ticinese architecture, nor certainly any Ticino School, in a conventional sense … this small group of architects offers no collective, general solutions. The phenomenon is international."[185] The role of the *Tendenzen* exhibition in 1975 had been precisely to "launch internationally a selection of Ticinese buildings as state-of-the-art products."[186] The discourse thus set into motion was predicated upon a niche product, concerning a tiny percentage of the buildings in the region:

> It is correct to highlight a few beautiful objects that were built here, but it is wrong to isolate the phenomenon of few avant-garde architects from Ticino, to make a myth out of it. The phenomenon was not born here, it merely found a particular expression here.[187]

184 Virgilio Gilardoni quoted in Bachmann, "Gründer, Schüler, Epigonen," 67.
185 Bachmann and Zanetti, "Die Moral und die Wirklichkeit," 184–185.
186 Bachmann and Zanetti, "Die Moral und die Wirklichkeit," 183. See also 179–81.
187 Bachmann and Zanetti, "Die Moral und die Wirklichkeit," 185.

The recent Ticinese architecture's unfulfilled ambitions for social and political transformation were of little to no consequence for its external audiences. Only local commentators such as Fumagalli and Gilardoni provided a multi-faceted critique of Ticinese architecture "as a cultural response to life in the province."[188] Immersed in this regional life and aware of its contradictions, their pronouncements could not and did not claim an Archimedean point of view, delivering instead pointed and balanced critiques with the authority of first-hand knowledge. By concentrating on the specifics of the phenomenon at hand, exposing its shortcomings and limited effectiveness, both the architect-journalist and the historian-archivist pointed to more open forms of architectural emancipation. In particular, the focus on architecture as a group formulation rendered it collectively intelligible—a practical and, ultimately, rational proposition.

Within Fumagalli's decades-long commentary on Ticinese architecture, his 1990 article "Europäische Zivilisation und örtliche Kultur am Beispiel Tessin" (European civilization and local culture using the example of Ticino) stands out as a rare direct response to Frampton's notion of critical regionalism. Operating within Frampton's culture–civilization dichotomy, Fumagalli pointed out that that the centripetal political momentum behind Switzerland's existence had been historically balanced with the centripetal forces of the "mother-cultures" of its three main linguistic regions: German, French, and Italian. Thus, he argued, Ticino architecture's deep roots in Italian culture and its participation in the Swiss discourse had to be viewed as sides of the same coin. For him, Ticino's perceived provincialism had been an "opportunity," motivating the architects to widen their horizons through travel and dialogues with other cultures, perhaps more so than metropolitan Zurich dwellers. Fumagalli once again rejected the term "Ticino School" as a

188 Paolo Fumagalli, "Europäische Zivilisation und örtliche Kultur am Beispiel Tessin," *disP—The Planning Review* 2, no. 103 (January 1990): 3–7, here 7.

misnomer for the "unity of intention" that had existed behind the production of the 1960s and 1970s. He did not see this professional knowledge as the intellectual product of few but rather as a gradual, partly accidental formation, originating in the theaters of built and theoretical production:

> Undoubtedly, in the 1970s Ticino assumed a leading status in the architectural field, compared with other regions of Switzerland. This hegemonic role does not, of course, refer to individual personalities (which also exist in other Swiss regions), but is linked to a new discourse that began to develop at that time. Numerous architects from Ticino have participated in this new discourse, consciously or unconsciously, some with mainly theoretical contributions, others with concrete buildings.[189]

Fumagalli was not alone in voicing this opinion. Later on, Bruno Reichlin critiqued in no uncertain terms the local advantages of association with internationally circulated theories. While "united in a mystical community through the grace of genius loci," he argued, Ticinese architects were forced to operate inside the restricted context granted by this very grace.[190] There was nothing mystical, he noted, in the harsh reality of competing against erstwhile partners and collaborators, all in a local context with limited opportunities for commissions. Attention from the outside, whether international or federal, whether in the form of publications or academic assignments, contributed to the creation of a professional hierarchy that ended up operating very much on the inside. The cultural currency it provided served to underline the parochial character of local professional networks:

189 Fumagalli, "Europäische Zivilisation," 7.
190 Bruno Reichlin, "Quand les architectes modernes construisent en montagne," in *L'invention de l'architecture alpine / Die Erfindung der alpinen Architektur*, ed. Reto Furter et al., Histoire des Alpes / Storia delle Alpi / Geschichte der Alpen, vol. 16 (Zurich: Chronos, 2011), 173–200, here 174.

As everyone knows, inside a regional socio-economic basin, the battle for survival imposes among the so-called "local" architects a subtle game of distinction, and hence the affiliation to external tendencies, groups and manifestos, cultural perfusions, the umbilical cord with the place of origin etc., meant to dazzle and turn green with envy the provincial architect next door.[191]

This statement points into a different direction than the idealistically titled "Gruppo Ticino" (Botta, Carloni, Galfetti, Ruchat-Roncati, and Snozzi) that had entered the competition for the EPFL campus in 1970. The course of time has shown that any possibility of a collective understanding, or indeed a representative group, had been temporary, one moment in a history being written. Despite all this, the later dissolution of the "Gruppo Ticino" and the divergent trajectories of its members did not erase the shared knowledge that this loose group had produced in the first place. A declared interest in the relation between buildings and their territory, cultural as well as topographic, continued to fuel the self-sufficiency of Ticinese architecture more than its historical or geographical status as a periphery.

For local commentators, the critical attention from the outside manifested itself in design as well as in theory. On the one hand, the formal emulation of buildings was seen as an almost inevitable development, but not one fully devoid of cynicism. Fumagalli's protest in 1986 at the "Xerox-culture" growing around Ticino architecture echoed Gilardoni's observation, one year earlier, that the built works were being subjected to intellectual, as well as formal, plagiarism: "One copies the external form and forgets the content of these original, non-reproducible works, the 'moral tension' from which they have emerged."[192] Interestingly, however, as Bachmann

191 Reichlin, "Quand les architects," 174.
192 Bachmann and Zanetti, "Die Moral und die Wirklichkeit," 184; cf. Fumagalli, "Tessiner Architekten."

also implied, this formal reproduction had also been propagated by younger "Hellenistic" generations within Ticino, not merely outside of it.

On the other hand, the theoretical readings that the buildings attracted, most notably those of Steinmann or Frampton, were of a different nature. They transferred the built matter into a realm of ideas, albeit at the cost of losing the finer grain of its historical circumstances. This process of de-materialization was, in fact, the place where the architecture could truly claim a degree of actual autonomy. Not only did the writing of theory allow the wider circulation of Ticinese architecture, but also, by extracting from it underlying principles, allowed its architectural replication—not as a formal plagiarism but as a design method. This method, based on the same set of interests as those stipulated by *Tendenza*, was subsequently adapted by other regional professional communities in the process of their own self-definition.

BETWEEN AUTONOMY AND REALISM

As already shown, the exhibition *Tendenzen: Neuere Architektur im Tessin* contained a paradox within the plural German form of its title. *Tendenzen* fulfilled a double role, acknowledging the translation potential of Italian theory while at the same time recognizing the intrinsic heterogeneity of the positions it opened up. In highlighting autonomy as an "essential common denominator" of the Ticinese works, curator Martin Steinmann touched upon one of *la Tendenza*'s main theoretical foci.[193] It is the contention of this book that the theory he constructed at the time acquired its own autonomy, departing from the agendas and circumstances of the works it sought to explain and at the same time allowing their circulation far beyond their immediate geographical and historical contexts. As a theoretical construct—that is, with a posited general validity—autonomy became a transgressive theme.

The autonomy of the theory addressed in this book is a parallel, separate phenomenon from the postulated autonomy of the built architecture it sought to explain. In its architectural sense, the notion of autonomy opens a complex and rather indeterminate field, which is here only briefly sketched out. Ernesto Rogers used the term as early as 1931, calling for the "autonomy of architecture from dogmas and cultural encrustations that have been forming over the course of time."[194] He argued for an architecture only accountable to a nominal set of "universal principles, common to all people of all times." Coming into its own during the late 1960s and early 1970s, the notion of autonomy included a plea for architecture's return to the historical and social context of the city. In 1969, Ezio Bonfanti programmatically posited that architecture and art should move away from the false distortions of local interests, obsolescent ideologies,

193 Steinmann, "Reality as History [1976a]," 155.
194 Ernesto Nathan Rogers, "Considerazioni sull'architettura moderna: Tesi per il corso di Organismi e storia dell'architettura, 1931," in *Architettura, misura e grandezza dell'uomo: scritti 1930–1969*, ed. Serena Maffioletti, vol. 5 (Padua: Poligrafo, 2010), 75–85, here 82.

and market demand.[195] Autonomy became associated with a *rappel a l'ordre*, meant to redraw the boundaries of the discipline. Architecture was thus to be set apart from a variety of possible rogue agents, alternatively described—depending on author and audience—as cultural dogmas, technocratic operations, or consumer culture. As such, it is not without irony that in the post-1968 Swiss political climate, Aldo Rossi's teachings at ETH Zurich were—despite his Marxist political orientation—viewed as an attempt to draw students back to an autonomous architectural field, at a safe distance from political activism.

This call to order extended from the practice of architecture to its analysis. In *The Architecture and the City*, Rossi mused:

> Sometimes I ask myself why architecture is not analyzed in these terms, that is, in terms of its profound value as a human thing that shapes reality and adapts material according to an aesthetic conception. It is in this sense not only the place of the human condition, but itself part of that condition.[196]

Even in Rossi's loose formulation, the notion of architectural autonomy was not meant as a withdrawal into purely aesthetic aspects of design. This proviso remains a consensus among critics. For Alan Colquhoun, architectural autonomy was "a meaningless phrase, since any principles of architecture are empty until embodied in an action, in the reality of a situation."[197] K. Michael Hays understood autonomy "as a relational concept, not as an isolationist position."[198]

195 Ezio Bonfanti, "Autonomia dell'architettura (Controspazio 1, 1969)," *Controspazio: Rivista bimestrale di architettura e urbanistica* 3 (June 1989): 12–20.

196 Rossi, *The Architecture of the City*, 34.

197 Alan Colquhoun, "A Way of Looking at the Present Situation," in *Modernity and the Classical Tradition: Architectural Essays* (Cambridge, MA: MIT Press, 1980), 193–99, here 198.

198 K. Michael Hays, "Prolegomenon for a Study Linking the Advanced Architecture of the Present to That of the 1970s through Ideologies of Media, the

The concept of autonomy most likely to have influenced the Swiss architectural discourses originated in 1960s Italy, where autonomy had never implied a "strategic retreat" of architecture from its socio-political and historical circumstances.[199] Pier Vittorio Aureli, exploring parallels between autonomy discourses in architecture and in politics in Italy, pointed out that

> autonomy entailed a refusal not of the reality of the emerging postindustrial city, but of the techno-utopian visions of the contemporary world …. For Rossi the possibility of autonomy occurred as a possibility of theory: of the reconstruction of the political, social, and cultural significations of urban phenomena divorced from any technocratic determinism.[200]

The concept of architectural autonomy that influenced the works and writings of thinkers and practitioners of the Italian *Tendenza* throughout the 1960s and 1970s was passed on to their Swiss counterparts in isolation from the political discourse that had originally accompanied it. Again, in this more strictly disciplinary sense, its circulation accelerated. The expanding range of architectural publications, exhibitions, teaching, and study trips that followed had a considerable impact on the subsequent architectural discussions in Europe and North America.[201] It was in this expanded context that one of the clearest explanations of what autonomy is, rather than what it is not, arose. In the early 1980s, Belgian art and architecture critic Geert Bekaert argued that auton-

Experience of Cities in Transition, and the Ongoing Effects of Reification," *Perspecta* 32 (2001): 101–107, https://doi.org/10.2307/1567287, here 102.

    199 Pier Vittorio Aureli, *The Project of Autonomy: Politics and Architecture within and against Capitalism* (New York: The Temple Hoyne Buell Center for the Study of American Architecture / Princeton Architectural Press, 2012), 12.

    200 Aureli, *Project of Autonomy*, 13.

    201 See for example Jean-Louis Cohen, *La coupure entre architectes et intellectuels, ou les enseignements de l'italophilie* (Brussels: Mardaga, 2015); Hays, "Prolegomenon."

omy in architecture resided not in an *a priori* attitude, but rather in moments: those short intervals when architects are fully focused on designing, when other (legitimate and valued) considerations or demands fade away. Thus,

> when they are busy with architecture, they are busy with nothing else, not with the social, the functional, the semiotic, the moral; which does not directly mean that they would not make social, functional buildings, loaded with meaning or moral sense. It is the essence of their preoccupation that it contains no reference but to itself, and it is in that preoccupation, that struggle with a reality that constitutes itself only in that struggle, that it comes down to it. The building, as a provisional and constantly renewable result of this preoccupation, is its own responsibility, possesses its own internal logic.[202]

So too does theory. As shown in the case of Steinmann's critical readings of Ticinese architecture, the theoretical discourse around architectural autonomy gradually acquired an autonomy of its own. The built architecture could never fully escape for longer than a few moments, during its design, from the historical conditions that enabled its existence. In contrast, the reflections it invited were free to divorce themselves from the interests and considerations that had animated the initial designs. The critical reception of the architecture thus gave rise to a new theoretical model, whose range of circulation depended on its capacity to be adopted by different attitudes and formal productions.

In turn, this theoretical model helped shape a design method, or rather a design toolkit, of widespread applicability based on processes of cultural adaptation and interpretation in each of its locations. The approach was strongly influ-

---

202 Geert Bekaert, "Het recht op architectuur (1980)," ed. Hilde Heynen, in *"Dat is architectuur": Sleutelteksten uit de twintigste eeuw* (Rotterdam: Uitgeverij 010, 2001), 541–45, here 544.

enced by the methodology of *Tendenza*, namely the four-fold engagement with the city, history, typology, and form—which acquired some of its earliest, most consistent built expressions in the contemporaneous architecture in Ticino. On the other hand—perhaps partly due to the dispersed urbanity of the Ticino—the static form-making derived from the observation of Italian historical monuments was balanced by an interest in ordinary environments and modest, familiar typologies. This, in turn, brought the architecture closer to the heading of realism, defined by a gray area between high culture and popular consumer culture.[203]

The autonomy of architecture, its relation to the city, and its use of the everyday as design source came together into a critical architectural approach. What Rossi had seen as an extension of autonomy from the practice to the analysis of architecture involved not only designer-practitioners but other reflective agents, including critics.[204] The design method that resulted from the combination of autonomy and realism was prominently articulated by a later generation of Northern Swiss, German-speaking architects, who had been directly influenced by Rossi's teaching at ETH Zurich.[205] This legacy is still perceptible in current Swiss production, in which Andrea Wiegelmann identified an oscillation between "two antipodes: on the one side an autonomous,

203 The issue of the connections and divergences between the Italian *Tendenza* and architectural realism is beyond the scope of this essay. It is, however, a charged one, not least because of Rossi's and his contemporaries' rejection of the neo-realism of an older generation of Italian practitioners, which nevertheless had impacted the cultural formation of Ticino architects in the 1950s and 1960. For Italian architectural neo-realism see Reichlin, "Figures of Neorealism"; Bruno Reichlin, "Figures of Neorealism in Italian Architecture (Part 2)," *Grey Room* 6 (2002): 110–33, https://doi.org/10.1162/152638102317406515. For the theoretical topos of realism as reflected in 1970s Swiss discourse see Davidovici, "Issues of Realism."

204 Rossi, *The Architecture of the City*, 34.

205 Following Rossi's teaching at ETH Zurich, for a few years his students continued to implement, with varying degrees of literalness, the Platonic forms and Northern Italian typologies of his architecture. Gradually however, they turned to the reworking of local formal and typological motifs, as seen in the ordinary yet atmospheric propositions of the Analoge Architektur studio, first set up by Fabio Reinhart then developed by Miroslav Šik.

self-referential, occasionally ironic architecture; on the other, an analogous position."[206] The combined appeal of autonomy and realism helped create a common design method.

A first step in this process is the morphological, typological, and historical analysis of a project's location: "taking stock of the site in terms of its architectural, and hence cultural, continuity."[207] Reading the complex architectural and cultural layers of their sites, in the early 1980s Northern Swiss architects started to produce heterogeneous designs that directly responded to their multifaceted contexts, such as Diener & Diener's St Alban Tal (1981–1986) (fig. 31) and Herzog & de Meuron's Photographic Studio Frei (1981–1982). Gradually, the earlier semiological subtexts and literal interpretations of historical forms became secondary to the seductive material qualities of constructed architecture. The late 1980s and early 1990s saw a shift towards the more unified, and at the same time more object-like buildings—as seen in Herzog & de Meuron's Ricola Storage in Laufen (1986) (fig. 32), Diener & Diener's Administration Building Picassoplatz in Basel (1987–93), Gigon/Guyer's Kirchner Museum in Davos (1986–1993), and Peter Zumthor's Thermal Baths in Vals (1996).

To be sure, to put such different buildings under the same heading amounts to no less than the theoretical flattening bemoaned everywhere else in this book. However, in the late 1980s and early 1990s, the construct of a "new" German-Swiss architecture was sufficiently coherent to an international community to acquire its own currency.[208] Its set of design strategies was indebted to Rossi's use of

206 Andrea Wiegelmann, "Justierungsprozesse," *archithese* 2 (2017): 74–79, here 74.

207 Martin Steinmann and Jacques Lucan, "Obsessions: Conversation entre Jacques Lucan et Martin Steinmann / Obsessions: Conversation between Jacques Lucan and Martin Steinmann," in *Matière d'art: Architecture contemporaine en Suisse / A Matter of Art: Contemporary Architecture in Switzerland*, ed. Institut de Théorie et d'Histoire de l'Architecture (Jacques Lucan and Bruno Marchand, et al.) (Basel: Birkhäuser, 2001), 8–25, here 10.

208 See, for example, Irina Davidovici, *Forms of Practice: German-Swiss*

31 Diener & Diener, residential buildings at St. Alban-Tal, Basel (1981–86). Here, the industrial history of the St. Alban-Tal was the basis for the combination of modern expression and function. The facades responded to different aspects of their immediate context, resulting in a multifaceted ensemble.

32 Herzog & de Meuron, Ricola Storage Building, Laufen (1986). The cladding of layered Eternit panels at varying intervals, supported by a partly visible timber substructure, wraps around the building, resulting in an abstract, unified presence.

analogy as a way to connect the architecture to the existing context while remaining distinct from it. Jacques Herzog's text from 1989, programmatic for his partnership with Pierre de Meuron, summarized this ambivalence towards historical reference:

> The relationship to pre-existing architectural and building form is unavoidable and important. Architecture has never arisen out of nothing. But there is no longer a mediatory tradition. This can also be seen in the way that contemporary architecture so often tries to fabricate a relationship to historical forms by means of quotation and with this practice penetrates no further than the surface of the eye's retina. What else can we do but carry within us all these images of the city, or pre-existing architecture and building forms and building materials, the smell of asphalt and car exhaust and rain, and to use our pre-existing reality as a starting point and to build our architecture in pictorial analogies? The utilization of these pictorial analogies, their dissection and recomposition into an architectural reality is a central theme in our work.[209]

In another methodological statement, Marcel Meili defined the work of his partnership and their contemporaries in terms of a "process of sedimentation of meanings into forms, resulting from the incessant repetition of everyday use," holding that "an architecture that could embody more general significations ... could be realized through a focus of design on

---

Architecture, 1980–2000, Second, revised and expanded edition (Zurich: gta Verlag, 2018).

209 Herzog & de Meuron, "Die verborgene Geometrie der Natur / The Hidden Geometry of Nature," in *Herzog & de Meuron 1978–1988: Das Gesamtwerk / The Complete Works*, ed. Gerhard Mack, vol. 1 (Basel: Birkhäuser, 1997), 207–211, here 207. Originally published as Jacques Herzog, "La geometria oculta de la naturaleza / The Hidden Geometry of Nature," in *Quaderns d'Arquitectura i Urbanisme: Geografies / Geographies*, ed. Josep Lluís Mateo, vols. 181/182 no. 9 (Barcelona: Collegi d'Arquitectes de Catalunya, 1989), 96–109.

the problem of form" and that "our incursions in the world of the ordinary and the everyday represented a search for collective meanings."[210] These formulations, ambiguously poised between the "we" of specific partnerships and a tentatively collective viewpoint, are specific of this generation of architects born in the 1950s and trained at ETH Zurich in the 1970s. At the same time, they give contour, yet again, to a range of positions independent of a regional index, and more generally associated with the Western post-industrial city. Incidentally, these positions are neither purely aesthetic nor autonomous. They are culturally specific and involved, which brings them towards the themes and concerns addressed by art-historical realism. The mixture of autonomy and realism points to the paradoxical nature of these notions in the architectural discourse.

The emergence of such spatially generic yet historically conditioned cultural formations was neither Swiss-wide nor constrained to Switzerland. Similar appeals to ordinary forms and practices as the basis for a common intelligibility can be identified, among others, in the designs and written statements of some British and Flemish architects. Among a few examples: early in their careers, British architects Jonathan Sergison and Stephen Bates located their position "somewhere between ideas and places," further defined by the concern with "the real and the ordinary … the manipulation of familiar images and forms in order to engage with the forces of association which we all hold within us."[211] And—uncharacteristic of the older generation to which he belonged—Tony Fretton anchored his personal interest in

210 Marcel Meili, "Ein paar Bauten, viele Pläne," in *Architektur in der Deutschen Schweiz, 1980–1990: Ein Katalog und Architekturführer / L'architecture récente en Suisse alémanique / L'architettura recente nella Svizzera Tedesca*, ed. Peter Disch (Lugano: ADV, 1991), 22–27, here 22. English translation in Davidovici, *Forms of Practice* [2012], 74.

211 Stephen Bates and Jonathan Sergison, "Somewhere Between Ideas and Places," in *Papers* (London: Sergison Bates architects, 2001), 2–7, here 2.

"mundane settings and material" in the observation of artistic practices from the 1960s onwards:

> I looked for an approach to making architecture that was socially and experientially engaging while speaking as freely about ideas as the visual arts. Robert Morris's sculptures and installations suggested that facts could be a source of compelling form, while Chris Burden's performance works let me understand the power of direct physical engagement with location. Dan Graham's writing, performance and installations showed very lucidly how popular culture could be interrogated to produce things of formal, experiential, and intellectual beauty.[212]

Fretton's words reveal how, even if the source of methodological inspiration differ—in this case being artistic discipline—the architecture was decided based on similar methods: the factual analysis of the site, the observation of popular culture, and the replication of artistic practices.

Oscillations between realism and autonomy are also identifiable in the Flemish architecture of the last few decades. The 2016 publication *Autonomous Architecture in Flanders* (fig. 33) posited that the designs, writings, and teaching of Marie-José Van Hee, Christian Kieckens, Marc Dubois, Paul Robbrecht, and Hilde Daem, all graduates of Sint-Lucas Ghent in 1974, had given rise to a "'silent school' in Flanders based on the "quest for an autonomous logic in architecture."[213] Accordingly, these architects

developed a research-based design attitude that was rooted in the study of architectural morphology and

212 Tony Fretton, "The Same Thing Said Four Times," in *Articles, Essays, Interviews and Out-Takes* (Heijningen: JAP SAM Books, 2018), 6–7.

213 Caroline Voet et al., eds., "Prologue," in *Autonomous Architecture in Flanders: The Early Works of Marie-José Van Hee, Christian Kieckens, Marc Dubois, Paul Robbrecht and Hilde Daem* (Leuven: Leuven University Press, 2016), 6–9, here 6.

33 Cover of *Autonomous Architecture in Flanders* (Leuven University Press, 2016)

typologies. Architecture was seen as an autonomous spatial phenomenon, charged with the perspectives of dwelling and experience. Artistry and craftsmanship were seen as central aspects of making architecture. In this manner they defined an architectural language that grew from spatial analyses, meticulous reflections on art, and an intense relationship with craftsmanship.[214]

Lara Schrijver defined the position of the Flemish "silencieux" as one in which "the social function of architecture—at least as approached by the modernists—took a backseat to concerns of space, of material and of design quality. Light, thickness, typology, became more central than the social concerns of their forebears."[215] This intra-disciplinary retreat was balanced with a sustained interest in ordinary urban contexts, methodologically influenced by the iconographic analyses of Robert Venturi, whether in his earlier *Complexity and Contradiction in Architecture* of 1966, or together with Denise Scott-Brown in *Learning from Las Vegas* of 1972. For practitioner Dirk Somers,

> A very Belgian reading of Venturi legitimises architecture as a play on reality. The solitary Belgian architect arms himself/herself with Venturi and presents himself/herself as a practical strategist that does not address inherent contradictions, but converts them into enthralling designs.[216]

214 Voet et al., "Prologue," 7.

215 Lara Schrijver, "Breathing Life into Bricks: The Legacy of the 1970s," in *Autonomous Architecture in Flanders: The Early Works of Marie-José Van Hee, Christian Kieckens, Marc Dubois, Paul Robbrecht, and Hilde Daem*, ed. Caroline Voet et al. (n.p.: Leuven University Press, 2016), 11–21, here 13.

216 Dirk Somers, "Venturi's Discipline," in *Autonomous Architecture in Flanders: The Early Works of Marie-José Van Hee, Christian Kieckens, Marc Dubois, Paul Robbrecht and Hilde Daem*, ed. Caroline Voet et al. (Leuven: Leuven University Press, 2016), 186–193, here 189.

Whether from Switzerland, Britain, or Flanders, these disparate statements converge on a referential and methodological field characterized by degrees of autonomy and realism. They do not, and cannot, represent a unique position, but rather constitute the shared horizon of a multitude of approaches of thinkers and practitioners at the end of the twentieth century, preoccupied with the analysis and justification of their formal productions on cultural grounds. While the notion of "reference" occurs repeatedly in their written statements, the references themselves are as diverse as the sites and their buildings. Thus the formal results are seldom comparable, although the design strategies are similar. Sometimes practices are adopted from the visual arts, while other times cultural continuity is highlighted, often in a high art/low culture tandem; or rigorous construction is brought into discussion as a counterpart to the lamented disappearance of traditional craftsmanship. Most often, the open-ended spectrum of "the" city is recalled, whether by itself or channeled through abstractions of its generic locations: the periphery, the high street, the neighborhood. As Somers put it in the Belgian context: "We allow America's post-War 'Main Street' and the 'Flemish steenweg' [built-up connecting road] to fraternise for a while with their similar car-oriented, shrill identities."[217] One of the most consistent interest of these scattered architects might be identified as the material they have inherited for working with: the damaged, discarded, and commonplace cityscapes of post-industrial economies.

217 Somers, "Venturi's Discipline," 189.

COMMUNITIES OF PRACTICE AS REGIONAL *TENDENZE*

Periodically, the architectural production of peripheral regions comes to the attention of mainstream cultural networks. This recognition manifests itself through an increase in the quantity and frequency of professional publications, group exhibitions, and guests teaching positions, which provide additional cultural capital for protagonists who initially were only active locally. This projection beyond their immediate area of activity comes at a cost. The more outwardly visible these actors become, the less they are able to maintain the erstwhile regional scope of the early works. Once aligned with a centrist value-system, they inevitably tend to reproduce it. Stalked by devotees, probed by critics, the architectural production of the nominal margin becomes an intellectual commodity efficiently consumed by the center.

The Ticinese architecture of the 1970s as discussed in the previous chapters represents only one rotation of this cycle. It illustrates an older phenomenon that continues to manifest itself: a particular sensitivity towards places and traditions, historically appropriated by the extensive postwar rethinking of modernist doctrines. Having taken root through 1960s Italian theory, the Ticinese design methodology was itself passed further on, contributing—through teaching, publications, and exhibitions—to the theoretical and professional flowering of German-Swiss production in the 1980s and beyond.[218] Related design approaches emerged, among others, in Portugal and Greece in the 1970s and 1980s, and further north, in Great Britain and Belgium, in the 1990s and 2000s. More recently, a similar critical attitude has gained visibility in France, in the work of young practices that use regional support networks, craftsmanship, and collective authorship to compensate for lack of access to official commissions.

This multi-generational, polycentric discourse of shared affinities can be visualized as a web of regional clusters. It emerges in specific cultural settings at certain times, subsequently gaining traction outside of these as they enter

218 See Davidovici, *Forms of Practice* [2012], 63–79.

wider international debates. And yet, across regions and across time, these clusters seem to communicate with each other—in whispers rather than shouts, barely acknowledged yet thorough as studies of precedent. It then becomes possible to trace the trajectories and genealogies of similar ideas in different locations. Their connections suggest that none of these "regional" cultures develops in isolation. Rather, shared values and attitudes attached to local factors are at the same time able to circulate internationally, creating dialogues between distinct architecture cultures. We may call these fluid common settings "communities of practice."

Communities of practice do not stand for one single aesthetic, style, or design approach. The built production is formally heterogeneous and can embody different ideological stances. Rather, communities of practice can be seen as a matter of collective affinities, describing universal conditions while bound to theaters of local practice. Their study allows a rough extrapolation of shared principles. Such communities of practice emerge from a collective rejection of establishment structures, construction industries, architectural mainstreams. The participating architects insist on building as the primary aim of architecture, generally achieved in small-scale, more controllable situations. They develop close connections with artisanal construction and find inspiration in ordinary environments. The use of local types, forms, and materials ensures the legibility of the buildings and their accord with their setting. The modesty of means is often adopted as an ethical position, which seems to exercise an irresistible appeal. Nevertheless, the adoption of such principles is coupled with their adaptation, both in the search for originality and in the avoidance of formal mimesis. The new buildings' familiarity is intentionally undercut by historical references and artistic strategies that serve to distance them from their surrounds and place them under the sign of (critical) interpretation. These communities of practice seem to communicate not only in terms of design approaches but also through a shared, often implied, belief in the ethical substrate of their works.[219]

Communities of practice are not only constituted through adherence to a set of common design methods or sensibilities. These are not ad hoc groupings of isolated individuals, but people producing and exchanging knowledge in shared professional and academic networks based on various forms of collaboration. Connections formed during the participants' training are particularly strong influences in the early years, formative stages when architects position themselves conceptually. Later in their careers, as architects seek reinvention, pursue individual trajectories, and gain access to international commissions, the collective regional index loses its relevance. This is turn renders the communities of practice highly unstable in any one place and generally only identifiable for short periods of time. Although they persistently reemerge elsewhere, the connection between an architectural production and one specific place tends to be outlived by the ongoing careers of erstwhile protagonists.

This recurring phenomenon is denoted by a vague, usually contested terminology. Despite its inherent problematic (since borders do not stop cultural influences), the regional index offers a seemingly clear criterion for collective definitions. This gives rise to umbrella terms as popular as they are misleading, often combining the qualification of novelty ("new," "recent," "contemporary," "emerging"), geo-cultural attributes with reference to regions (Italian, Ticinese, Portuguese, Belgian, Flemish, Spanish, Swiss), or cities (London, New York), and collective nouns (school, group, generation). Terms anchored to historical dates, such as the Flemish "Generation '74" (referring to the vintage year when Marie-José Van Hee, Christian Kieckens, Marc Dubois, Paul Robbrecht, and Hilde Daem graduated from Sint-Lucas in Ghent) and the "Swiss architects born around 1950" (associated mostly

---

219 Bachmann and Zanetti, "Die Moral und die Wirklichkeit," 184.

but not exclusively with Jacques Herzog, Pierre de Meuron, Roger Diener, Marcel Meili, Christian Sumi, and Marianne Burkhalter) inevitably include some architects that have nothing to do with the original impetus, while excluding others (younger or older) that do. Moreover, the meaning of such composites is understandably unstable from one decade to the next, since nothing is forever "new," local indexes are subject to political redefinition, and "schools" or "groups" are often external projections resisted from within. More resilient, albeit notoriously vague, have proven the euphemistic terms used to describe these communities of practice: not only "la Tendenza" in Italy and *"Tendenzen"* in Ticino, but also "gritty Brits" in the United Kingdom or "les silencieux" in Belgium (fig. 34).[220] Often coined in the context of fluctuating and temporary collective settings such as group exhibitions or publications, these terms are often rejected by the very people they are meant to represent. And yet, the need for finding a specific terminology in the first place signals their newfound relevance in the International discourse.

A common element for the various communities of practice is a strong element of reflection, which manifests itself, in parallel to the buildings, in a written production of essays, monographs, exhibitions. Their existence depends on what David Schön called "the reflective practitioner" as one who "shifts from embracing freedom of choice to acceptance of implications, from involvement in the local units to a distanced consideration of the resulting whole, and from a stance of tentative exploration, to one of commitment."[221] The reflective practitioner's work oscillates between universal

---

220 The term "gritty Brits" (denoting Adjaye Associates, Caruso St John Architects, FAT [Fashion Architecture Taste], Niall McLaughlin Architects, muf and Sergison Bates architects) was coined during the eponymous exhibition *Gritty Brits: New London Architecture* at the Heinz Architectural Center, Carnegie Museum of Art, Pittsburgh, January 20 to June 3, 2007, curated by Raymond Ryan and Iain Sinclair. See Raymund Ryan and Iain Sinclair, eds., *Gritty Brits: New London Architecture* (Pittsburgh: Carnegie Museum of Art, 2006). For 'les silencieux' see Schrijver, "Breathing Life into Bricks," 12-13.

221 Donald A. Schön, "Design as a Reflective Conversation with the Situ-

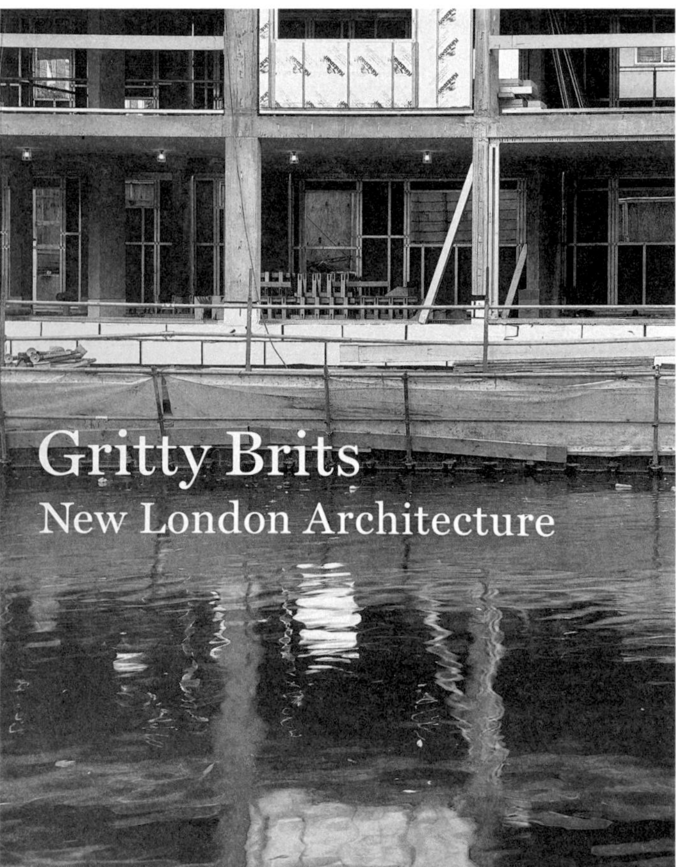

34 A London 'tendency'? Cover of *Gritty Brits: New London Architecture*, edited by Raymund Ryan and Iain Sinclair (Pittsburgh: Carnegie Museum of Art, 2006)

and locally specific constructions of meaning: as a "global experiment, [it] is also a reflective conversation with the situation."[222]

Architecture's engagement with host cultures and environments is mostly addressed at a conceptual level. Abstract notions such as typologies, historical references, meanings, and signs are emphasized. Moments of reflection and the development of positions occur in isolation (as writing is usually solitary) but at the same time almost inevitably in dialogue with a wider context. Communities of practice depend to a great extent upon the participants' ability to navigate the landscape of professional recognition through the channels of publications, lectures, exhibitions, and teaching. Not all of these participants are equally inclined to write about what they do. They do not all have the same sources, training, or skill sets. They are unlikely to get together and declare their henceforth adherence to a like-minded professional community. But they implicitly know that they are part of a sustaining network, even while competing against each other for individual commissions. The group architectural exhibition is a typical example of an explicit reflective endeavor, whereby gathering and comparing contemporaneous works and practices helps articulate shared theoretical platforms and encourage the emergence of collective awareness.[223]

Common patterns and stages can be discerned in the formation of such genealogies of local discourses. Initially a design method is articulated, or adapted, by a cluster of critical practices, in a tentative constellation of isolated projects or buildings. This attracts the attention of critics and other re-

ation," in *The Reflective Practitioner: How Professionals Think in Action* (Abington: Routledge, 2017), 76–104, here 102.

222 Schön, "Design as a Reflective Conversation," 103.

223 For the case of recent Belgian-Flemish architectural culture, see Sofie De Caigny and Katrien Vandermarliere, "More Than Punctual Interventions: Cultural Events, Competitions and Public Debate as Impetus for Architectural Culture in Flanders, 1974–2000," in *Autonomous Architecture in Flanders: The Early Works of Marie-José Van Hee, Christian Kieckens, Marc Dubois, Paul Robbrecht, and Hilde Daem*, ed. Caroline Voet et al. (Leuven: Leuven University Press, 2016), 49–61.

flective practitioners; dialogues ensue in publications, group exhibitions, collaborations, and teaching. In turn, these lead to the consolidation of the initial approach, which becomes generalized as modus operandi among peers and younger generations. Around this time, the initial trajectories diverge as actors go in different directions. Professional recognition and critical interest are unevenly distributed. In the end, communities of practice persist in many ways other than practice. Through parallel written productions of theory and criticism, they tend to linger in the architectural imagination long after their perceived communal aspects have withered away. Communities of practice attract the creation of autonomous theoretical constructs, which mediate the transfer of related methods between cultural contexts and between architectural generations. The fascination with theoretical implications tends, however, to overlook the place-bound political and pragmatic considerations that shape the professional culture of these ephemeral clusters.

EPILOGUE

Built and written architectures alternate in cycles of production and consumption—not only of design, but also of theory. What had started as a number of buildings in 1960s and 1970s Ticino—in part influenced by the theoretical input of Italian contemporaries, in part by the architects' own Modernist formations—ended up being themselves repackaged through theory, which led to their wider circulation. In turn, this theoretical production gave rise to a design method which contributed to subsequent architectural developments in Switzerland and abroad. At the same time, the case of Ticinese architecture has illustrated how the distillation of theory from built projects necessarily edits out the nuanced understanding of their context. Theoretical production divorces architectural knowledge from the historically specific conditions that enabled it in the first place. Theory operates most readily in a universally valid field of references, legible mostly from within the discipline. It necessitates an abstracted reading of built architecture and propagates on the basis of suppressing the specific in the search for general principles that can then be equally applied to different tasks and contexts. The more universal these principles, the more suited to their wider dissemination they prove to be. The local specificities of (inevitably messy) contexts muddy the clarity of architectural reflection.

The autonomy of architecture as a formal production is therefore paralleled by the autonomy of theory as a discourse. The critical reception of Ticinese architecture in the 1970s and 1980s has shown how the decontextualized reading of the buildings enabled them to be imported into international debates. Stripped to what was deemed fundamental by the critics, the architecture became a replicable formal and methodological model, able to appeal to ever-wider professional circles. The rising interest in the recent Ticinese architecture was enabled by its attractiveness to extraneous theoretical readings.

In its original sense, coined as theorized in Italy, *tendenza* represented an attempt to render architecture intelligible. This endeavor was collective inasmuch as its protagonists sought to engage in their work within the cultural horizon they inevitably shared: training, publications, the professional field. A similar tangle of relationships engulfed the Ticinese architects who were historically able to put its theories into practice in a different territory, under a set of historically different, arguably more fertile conditions for design and building. It is in this respect that the regional index matters: as the node of multiple factors that architecture—no matter how autonomous—is nevertheless dependent upon. No singular artistic vision, no single regional school develops in isolation, but is situated within social and professional networks. Cultures, including architectural ones, are intrinsically collective.

As the work of some local thinkers has shown, the proper grasp of the factors specific to the location can change, even rectify, the interpretation of the built works. But critique also operates politically. From outside of events, the readings of external critics rely upon a system of peripheries, where architecture is produced, and centers, where it is consumed. Theory, in this respect, becomes an extractive process, with the built architecture as resource. In the ecology of professional interdependencies, the sociocultural capital surplus that results benefits architect and critic alike. Critical attention brings in more commissions; more publications bring prestige. These markers of professional and academic success provide access to political power and thus can, ideally, fulfill the potential of an effectively transformative architecture, in social and cultural terms. Local intellectual production—circumscribed by language, regional specificity, and local knowledge—is less equipped to operate in the context of the general discourse. Who is interested in reading about the minutiae of practice, the divergent agendas and power structures within a competition jury, the often-tribal structures of local politics that lead to commissions? Moreover, how can this mass of detail ever be distilled into a theoretical proposition? Which leads to another set of questions: Is the suppression of historical detail a precondition for the architectural discourse? How can we produce theories of architecture that do not flatten buildings to the thickness of a page?

Aurelio Galfetti's sensitive yet quietly radical refurbishment of the Castelgrande in Bellinzona was completed in 1992, contributing to the site's UNESCO listing in 2000 (fig. 35).[224] Alongside a few smaller jewels, such as Livio Vacchini's gymnasium in Losone (1997), it represented a last hurrah of the Ticinese architecture that in the 1970s had been called "recent." By this time, the initial energy of the production had largely abated. Subsequent generations dealt with a different set of practice conditions: an intimidating array of elderly mentors, a shrinking pool of opportunities for public commissions, less visionary politicians, and increasingly risk-averse clients. By the mid-1980s, critical attention had shifted to German-Swiss architecture north of the Alps. The work of this new generation of practitioners remained clearly marked by design tools they had acquired during their formative years, especially those developed by Rossi (and, to a certain extent, the Ticinese architects). In its own ways—starkly reductive, conceptual, sensuous, yet formally restrained—the German-Swiss production of the 1980s and 1990s completed the intellectual trajectory of the *Tendenza*, developing further along the lines of the tenets of architectural autonomy.

The fascination with the idea of the city as an artifact continued to hold sway. However, the multitude of micro-cultures and regional rivalries in German-speaking

224 For the role of the Castelgrande refurbishment in the context of Ticinese architecture, see Stanislaus von Moos, "Castello propositivo: Identität, Erinnerung und Monumentalität im Tessin, 1970–2000," in *Nicht Disneyland: Und andere Aufsätze über Modernität und Nostalgie* (Zurich: Scheidegger & Spiess, 2004), 113–28.

35 Aurelio Galfetti, Castelgrande refurbishment, Bellinzona (1982–1992):
public entry to the elevator shaft cut inside the rock

Switzerland offered critics fewer opportunities for overarching narratives as durable, or compelling, as those which Ticino had enabled. In the late 1990s, Frampton briefly revisited the German-Swiss scene with a pertinent critique, contrasting two of its most prominent protagonists at this time: the partnership of Herzog & de Meuron and Peter Zumthor.[225] Once again, his argument identified in these bodies of work an underlying belief in the autonomy of the architectural artifact, supplemented by material references that served to embed it into its context.[226]

The main critical narratives in Ticinese architectural historiography might be posited as external, highly selective, international readings versus less circulated, inclusive, and precise local ones. In other words, the historiography is characterized by the duality of concise theoretical constructs versus detailed situated perspectives. In terms of their effectiveness, the former category had the greater impact. Various external arguments have rewritten local Ticinese architecture as a vehicle for independent theoretical agendas. These compelling narratives significantly raised its international profile and aligned it with a global discourse, at the cost of abstracting it from the deeper context that had defined it. This autonomy, of theories more than of architecture, mirrored the universalizing claim of the classical tradition. The annexation of Ticinese production to alternatively Italian, German, and Anglo-Saxon cultures implicitly reinforced a Eurocentric rather than regional perspective.

Steinmann's association of Ticinese architecture with the themes of Italian neo-rationalism, and Frampton's subsequent reading of it in terms of critical regionalism, were two

225 Kenneth Frampton, "Minimal Moralia: Reflections on Recent Swiss German Production," in *Labour, Work and Architecture: Collected Essays on Architecture and Design* (London: Phaidon, 2002), 324–31.

226 For an extended commentary on Frampton's essay, see Irina Davidovici, "The Dilemma of Authenticity I: Swiss Architecture between Ethical Intent and Aesthetic Object (2006)," in *Complexity of the Ordinary International Conference, Technion* (Haifa, 2006).

external interventions that profoundly affected not only its outer perception but also its inner development. The *Tendenzen* construct instilled a sense of collective self-awareness, endowing a number of Ticinese architects with cultural capital and, later on, political agency. Precisely on account of its distance, Steinmann's intellectualized analysis of Ticinese architecture provided an influential redefinition of architectural realism. As editor K. Michael Hays commented when including his key text in the prestigious anthology *Architecture Theory since 1968*, Steinmann's reading offered "an immanent reality of architecture that is both positive and as profoundly historical and social as history and society themselves."[227]

In contrast to the international clamor it had caused, Frampton's characterization of Ticinese architecture as critical regionalism received a markedly more subdued reception in the place of its origin. Its insights pale in comparison with the more nuanced and far less visible readings of the work that emerged both within Ticino—notably those of historian Virgilio Gilardoni and architects Tita Carloni and Paolo Fumagalli—and in the rest of Switzerland—Martin Tschanz, André Bideau, Nott Caviezel, and again an older Steinmann come to mind. Published mostly in Italian and German, these interpretations renounced tight theoretical frameworks in favor of depicting a pluralist scenery of diverging personalities and agendas, loosely if fundamentally connected by a collective conscience.

Continuing his research at the interface between design and criticism, Martin Steinmann became the leading commentator on the architecture of the German-Swiss architectural generation born in the 1950s.[228] As editor, together with Irma Noseda, of the journal *archithese* between 1980 and 1986, he strategically thematized discussions connect-

227 K. Michael Hays, introduction to Steinmann, "Reality as History [1998]," here 246.

228 For a full bibliography of his writings up to 2002, see Martin Steinmann, *Forme forte: Écrits / Schriften, 1972–2002* (Basel: Birkhäuser, 2003), 298–300.

ing contemporaneous practice and reflection onto the past (fig. 36). With issues focused on less-known modernists at home and abroad, on contemporary issues and materials, and with regular "state of affairs" surveys, *archithese* shaped a professional discourse marked by the attention to detail and nuance characteristic of an insider to the scene. Through its mix of international and home-grown themes, Steinmann's editorship of *archithese* anticipated, and to a great extent eclipsed, the international critiques of German-Swiss architecture for decades to come (fig. 37). Gradually, Steinmann's earlier theoretical focus on semiology and realism gave way to an interest in perception, culminating in the notion of "*forme forte*," widely understood as a 1990s version of architectural autonomy.[229]

Examining the cultural resonance of images and built forms, Steinmann endorsed the articulation of concepts as a way to sustain formal production. This strategy, already fully formed by 1975, left an indelible mark on the conceptual turn of subsequent Swiss architecture. His surveys of contemporary architecture covered projects of many stripes, from the high-tech projects of Theo Hotz to the deliberately ordinary houses of Michael Alder; but most actively he promoted the work of emergent practices such as Herzog & de Meuron, Peter Zumthor, Burkhalter Sumi, Gigon/Guyer, and, in the most detail, Diener & Diener.[230] Together with Roger Diener, in 1995 Steinmann coauthored *Das Haus und die Stadt*, an exhibition catalogue of urban master plans which, similarly to the *Tendenzen* catalogue before, acquired a cult following among younger architects (fig. 38).[231] In the late

229 Martin Steinmann, "La Forme Forte: En deçà des signes," *Faces* 19 (1991): 4–13; see also Steinmann and Kurz, "Experienced Space," 120.

230 For an overview of these contributions see Steinmann, *Forme forte*, in particular "Neuere Architektur in der Deutschen Schweiz" (1991), 93–109; "Die Gegenwärtigkeit der Dinge" (1994), 111–31; and "Die Unterwäsche von Madonna" (1997), 209–25.

231 Martin Steinmann and Roger Diener, *Das Haus und die Stadt / The House and the City: Diener & Diener—Städtebauliche Arbeiten / Urban Studies* (Basel: Birkhäuser, 1995).

36 Cover of *archithese* 5 (1985), *Bauen mit Holz / Construire en bois* (Building in timber), edited by Martin Steinmann. The issue focused on the cultural associations of timber construction in 1980s German-Swiss architecture.

37 Cover of *archithese* 1 (1986), *Stand der Dinge / Etat des choses* (The state of things), edited by Martin Steinmann. This overview of contemporaneous German-Swiss architecture was fronted by Diener & Diener's project for Basler Kantonalbank (1986), whose elevations mirrored different urban conditions.

1990s, as the temporary perceived unity of Swiss architecture was challenged by a growing divergence of approaches, Steinmann continued to insist that design decisions must remain based on some form of explicit intellectual positioning. As such, his written oeuvre about built things contains an interesting paradox. By compelling architects to articulate their ideas in writing, he became associated with a theoretical stance that appropriated their built works into the construction of its own legitimacy.[232] Like the design methods he encouraged architects to articulate, Steinmann used criticism to "build" its own site.

As Fumagalli had done in Ticino, Steinmann became involved in the politics of the built environment in the years before his death in 2022. Whereas Fumagalli had been the president of Ticino's *Commissione cantonale del paesaggio* between 2007 and 2013, Steinmann fronted the Basel *Stadtbildkommission* (the Basel-Cityscape Commission) between 2013 and 2018. The concern with the inner agendas of local practice cast him further away from the international limelight. Towards the end of a distinguished career, he noted that the early success of *Tendenzen* had never been replicated.[233]

In 2009, Steinmann publicly reflected on the 1970s Ticinese architecture in a lecture at the Accademia in Mendrisio–the actual "school of the Ticino" that the *Tendenzen* exhibition had, indirectly, rendered possible. Having never before used the term in his earlier writings on Ticino, Steinmann entitled his talk "L'école tessinoise à la sortie des

232 After retiring from teaching architecture at EPF Lausanne (1987–2007), Steinmann returned to practice in a collaborative project with Diener & Diener and Felix Josef Müller for the expansion of the Stadtmuseum Aarau (2007–2015). He served as president of the Basel Stadtbildkommission, which controls the design quality of architectural projects in the city, between 2013 and 2018. In 2016, he was awarded the prestigious Meret Oppenheim Prize for his contributions to Swiss architecture.

233 See Steinmann and Kurz, "Experienced Space," 120.

38 Cover of Martin Steinmann and Roger Diener, *Das Haus und die Stadt /
The House and the City* (Birkhäuser: Basel, 1995). Conceived as an exhibition
catalogue, this book had a lasting impact on younger generations of Swiss
practitioners.

classes" (The School of the Ticino at the end of the day).[234] He explained:

> I've never spoken of a "Ticino school." If I did use this term in the title of my talk this evening, it's because it conjures up an image that I like: the moment when the bell signals the end of school, the classroom doors open, the pupils come out into the courtyard, they shout, they run, they leave, sometimes sharing some of the way home. ... Indeed, the courtyard, to keep with the image, was suddenly full of Ticino architects. The 1975 exhibition marked what is known in French as *la sortie des classes*. And the noise in the courtyard? It was the magazines that did it, following the exhibition, for years, the critics ... and the "critics' critics."[235]

The "noise in the courtyard" has offered occasion for the inquiries of the present essay. Thanks to its focus on a clearly defined, limited situation, the critical reception of the Ticinese architecture has allowed the (partial) reconstruction of the paper apparatus through which theoretical writing positions itself with respect to the designed and built architecture, both before and after the event. The uneven commentaries, corresponding to the highs and lows of the discourse, have offered a glimpse into the formation of architectural culture and the production of autonomous, non-contingent theory. At the end of the day, when the protagonists have departed and the courtyard goes quiet, this is what remains.

234 Martin Steinmann, "L'école tessinoise à la sortie des classes," lecture given on the occasion of the opening of the exhibition *Il Bagno di Bellinzona* at the Accademia di Architettura, Mendrisio, September 17, 2009. Published in Italian translation as Steinmann, "La Scuola ticinese."
235 Steinmann, "La Scuola ticinese," 35.

ANNEX

BIBLIOGRAPHY

a+u / Architecture and Urbanism. "Residences." 69 (September 1976): 23–145.

Abteilung für Architektur, Technikum Winterthur Ingenieurschule, ed. *Neuere Architektur im Tessin: Exkursion Herbst 1982—Eine Dokumentation.* Winterthur: Technikum Winterthur Ingenieurschule, 1982.

Angélil, Marc, and Cary Siress. "Operation Switzerland: How to Build a Clockwork Nation." In *Mirroring Effects: Tales of Territory*, 707–94. Berlin: Ruby Press, 2019.

Aureli, Pier Vittorio. *The Project of Autonomy: Politics and Architecture within and against Capitalism.* New York: The Temple Hoyne Buell Center for the Study of American Architecture / Princeton Architectural Press, 2012.

Bachmann, Dieter, ed. *Du: Die Zeitschrift der Kultur* 585 (November 1989).

Bachmann, Dieter, ed. *Du: Die Zeitschrift der Kultur* 615 (May 1992).

Bachmann, Dieter, ed. "Ein Partisan: Editorial." *Du: Die Zeitschrift der Kultur* 585 (November 1989): 11–17.

Bachmann, Dieter. "Gründer, Schüler, Epigonen." *Du: Die Zeitschrift für Kunst und Kultur* 546 (August 1986): 66–72.

Bachmann, Dieter, and Gerardo Zanetti, eds. *Architektur des Aufbegehrens: Bauen im Tessin.* Basel: Birkhäuser, 1985.

Bachmann, Dieter, and Gerardo Zanetti, eds. "Die Moral und die Wirklichkeit: Ein Gespräch mit dem Historiker Virgilio Gilardoni." In *Architektur des Aufbegehrens: Bauen im Tessin*, 175–86. Basel: Birkhäuser, 1985.

Bates, Stephen, and Jonathan Sergison. "Somewhere Between Ideas and Places." In *Papers*, 2–7. London: Sergison Bates architects, 2001.

Bekaert, Geert. "Het recht op architectuur (1980)." Edited by Hilde Heynen. In *"Dat is architectuur": Sleutelteksten uit de twintigste eeuw*, 541–45. Rotterdam: Uitgeverij 010, 2001.

Bideau, André. "Tessiner und andere Tendenzen / La Tendenza au Tessin et ailleurs / The Tendenza in the Ticino and elsewhere." *Werk, Bauen + Wohnen* 84, no. 12 (1997): 22–36.

Boesiger, Willy. *Le Corbusier: Les dernières œuvres / The Last Works / Die letzten Werke.* Vol. 8. Zurich: Les Editions d'architecture Artemis, 1965.

Boga, Thomas, ed. *Tessiner Architekten: Bauten und Entwürfe, 1960–1985 / Ticino Architects, Buildings and Projects, 1960–1985 / Architetti Ticinesi, Edifici e progetti, 1960–1985.* Zurich: ETH Zurich, 1986.

Bonfanti, Ezio. "Autonomia dell'architettura (Controspazio 1, 1969)." *Controspazio: Rivista bimestrale di architettura e urbanistica* 3 (June 1989): 12–20.

Botta, Mario. "Academic High School in Morbio Inferiore: Intervention Criteria and Design Objectives." In *Tendenzen: Neuere Architektur im Tessin*, Second edition, edited by Martin Steinmann and Thomas Boga, 160. Zurich: ETH Zurich, 1976.

Botta, Mario, et al. *Scuola Politecnica Federale Losanna—Piano Direttore—Relazione.* Genestrerio: no publisher, 1970.

Brown-Manrique, Gerardo. *Architekturführer Tessin und Lombardei: Die neuen Bauten.* Translated by Cornelia Berg-Brandl. Stuttgart: Hatje, 1990.

Brown-Manrique, Gerardo. *The Ticino Guide.* New York: Princeton Architectural Press, 1989.

Bukowski, Manfred, and Roland Ostertag. *Tessin: Bergdörfer und neue Villen—Dokumentation einer Studiengruppe des Fachbereichs Architektur der Technischen Universität Braunschweig.* Third edition. Braunschweig: TU Braunschweig, 1979.

Burckhardt, Lucius, and Diego Peverelli. "Sieben Projektaufträge für die ETH-L in Dorigny." *Das Werk:*

Architektur und Kunst / L'Oeuvre: Architecture et Art 57, no. 10 (1970): 646–61.

Buzzi, Giovanni. "Costruzione del territorio e spazio urbano nel cantone Ticino: Rossis Beitrag zur Untersuchung der Kulturlandschaft." In *Aldo Rossi und die Schweiz: Architektonische Wechselwirkungen*, edited by Ákos Moravánszky and Judith Hopfengärtner, 97–106. Zurich: gta Verlag, 2011.

Campi, Mario, Franco Pessina, and Niki Piazzoli. "Montebello Castle in Bellinzona." In *Tendenzen: Neuere Architektur im Tessin*, Second edition, edited by Martin Steinmann and Thomas Boga, 162. Zurich: ETH Zurich, 1976.

Carbonell, Adrià, and Roi Salgueiro Barrio. "Notes on Aldo Rossi's Geography and History; the Human Creation." *Cartha* 2, no. 18 (2016): 36–37.

Carloni, Tita. "Tra conservazione e innovazione: Appunti sull'architettura nel canton Ticino dal 1930 al 1980." In *50 anni di architettura in Ticino, 1930-1980: Quaderno della rivista tecnica della Svizzera Italiana*, edited by Peter Disch, 4–11. Bellinzona-Lugano: Grassico Pubblicità, 1983.

Caruso, Alberto. "Architettura e politica." *Archi: rivista svizzera di architettura, ingegneria e urbanistica / Schweizerische Zeitschrift für Architektur, Ingenieurwesen und Stadtplanung* 6 (2014): 47–48.

Caviezel, Nott. "Switzerland since the 1970s: From Ticino Tendenza to Pluralism." In *Architectural Epicentres: Inventing Architecture, Intervening in Reality*, edited by Petra Čeferin and Cvetka Požar, 90–103. Ljubljana: Arhitekturni Muzej, 2008.

Ceschi, Raffaello. *Geschichte des Kantons Tessin*. Frauenfeld: Huber, 2003.

Cohen, Jean-Louis. *La coupure entre architectes et intellectuels, ou les enseignements de l'italophilie*. Brussels: Mardaga, 2015.

Colquhoun, Alan. "A Way of Looking at the Present Situation." In *Modernity and the Classical Tradition: Architectural Essays*, 193–99. Cambridge, MA: MIT Press, 1980.

Colquhoun, Alan. "Regionalism 1." In *Collected Essays in Architectural Criticism*, 280–286. London: Black Dog, 2009.

Dal Busco, Fabio, and Chiara Orelli. "Virgilio Gilardoni." In *Historisches Lexikon der Schweiz (HLS)*. https://hls-dhs-dss.ch/de/articles/010181/2007-09-06/.

Dal Co, Francesco. "Critique d'une exposition." *L'architecture d'aujourd'hui* 190 (1977): 58–60.

Davidovici, Irina. *Forms of Practice: German Swiss Architecture, 1980–2000*. Zurich: gta Verlag, 2012.

Davidovici, Irina. *Forms of Practice: German-Swiss Architecture, 1980–2000*. Second, revised and expanded edition. Zurich: gta Verlag, 2018.

Davidovici, Irina. "Issues of Realism: Archithese, Postmodernism and Swiss Architecture, 1971–1986." In *Mediated Messages: Periodicals, Exhibitions and the Shaping of Postmodern Architecture*, edited by Véronique Patteeuw and Léa-Catherine Szacka, 101–20. London: Bloomsbury Visual Arts, 2018. https://doi.org/10.5040/9781350046207.

Davidovici, Irina. "The Background of Culture." In *Forms of Practice: German-Swiss Architecture 1980–2000*, 21–39. Zurich: gta Verlag, 2012.

Davidovici, Irina. "The Dilemma of Authenticity I: Swiss Architecture between Ethical Intent and Aesthetic Object (2006)." In *Complexity of the Ordinary International Conference, Technion*. Haifa, 2006.

Davidovici, Irina, and Katrin Albrecht. "Konzept Convivium." *Werk, Bauen + Wohnen* 104, no. 12 (2017): 8–19.

De Caigny, Sofie, and Katrien Vandermarliere. "More Than Punctual Interventions: Cultural Events, Competitions and Public Debate as Impetus for Architectural Culture in Flanders, 1974–2000." In *Autonomous Architecture in Flanders: The Early Works of Marie-José Van Hee, Christian Kieckens, Marc Dubois, Paul Robbrecht, and Hilde Daem*, edited by Caroline Voet, Katrien Vandermarliere, Sofie De Caigny, and Lara Schrijver, 49–61. Leuven: Leuven University Press, 2016.

Deleuze, Gilles. *Difference and Repetition*. Translated by Paul Patton. London: Bloomsbury, 2014.

Disch, Peter, ed. *50 anni di architettura in Ticino, 1930–1980: Quaderno della rivista tecnica della Svizzera italiana*. Bellinzona: Grassico Pubblicità, 1983.

Disch, Peter, ed. *Architektur in der deutschen Schweiz, 1980–1990: Ein Katalog und Architekturführer / L'architecture récente en Suisse alémanique / L'architettura recente nella Svizzera Tedesca*. Second edition. Lugano: ADV, 1991.

Disch, Peter, Jacques Lucan, and Paolo Fumagalli. *Architettura recente nel Ticino, 1980–1995 / Neuere Architektur im Tessin, 1980–1995: Con un riassunto degli anni 1930–1980 / Mit einer Zusammenfassung der Jahre 1930–1980*. Lugano: ADV, 1996.

Draeger, Wolfhart, and Dieter Bachmann, eds. *Du: Die Zeitschrift für Kunst und Kultur* 546 (August 1986).

Driessche, Maarten Van Den, and Dirk Somers. "A Conversation Between Friends." In *Bovenbouw Architectuur: Living the Exotic Everyday*, edited by Dirk Somers, Maarten Van Den Driessche, and Bart Verschaffel, 145–202. Antwerp: Flanders Architecture Institute, 2019.

Durisch, Giancarlo. "House in Riva San Vitale." In *Tendenzen: Neuere Architektur im Tessin*, Second edition, edited by Martin Steinmann and Thomas Boga, 160–61. Zurich: ETH Zurich, 1976.

Eggener, Keith L. "Placing Resistance: A Critique of Critical Regionalism." *Journal of Architectural Education* 55, no. 4 (2002): 228–37.

Ente ticinese per il turismo, ed. *Itinerari di architettura moderna in Ticino / Auf den Spuren der modernen Architektur im Tessin*. Bellinzona: Ente ticinese per il turismo, 1989.

Forster, Kurt W. "Architektur vor dem Verstummen retten." In *Aldo Rossi und die Schweiz: Architektonische Wechselwirkungen*, edited by Ákos Moravánszky and Judith Hopfengärtner, 119–130. Zurich: gta Verlag, 2011.

Forty, Adrian. *Words and Buildings: A Vocabulary of Modern Architecture*. London: Thames & Hudson, 2000.

Frampton, Kenneth. "Critical Regionalism: Modern Architecture and Cultural Identity." Chap. 5 in *Modern Architecture: A Critical History*, Fourth edition, 314–27. London: Thames & Hudson, 2007.

Frampton, Kenneth. *L'altro Movimento Moderno*. Edited by Ludovica Molo. Translated by Maddalena Ferrara. Mendrisio: Mendrisio Academy Press, 2015.

Frampton, Kenneth. "Mario Botta and the School of the Ticino." *Oppositions* 14 (1978): 1–25.

Frampton, Kenneth. "Minimal Moralia: Reflections on Recent Swiss German Production." In *Labour, Work and Architecture: Collected Essays on Architecture and Design*, 324–31. London: Phaidon, 2002.

Frampton, Kenneth. *Modern Architecture: A Critical History*. Fourth edition. London: Thames & Hudson, 2007.

Frampton, Kenneth. "Prospects for a Critical Regionalism." *Perspecta* 20 (1983): 147–162.

Frampton, Kenneth. "Ten Points on an Architecture of Regionalism: A Provisional Polemic." In *Architectural*

Regionalism: Collected Writings on Place, Identity, Modernity, and Tradition, edited by Vincent Canizaro, 375–85. New York: Princeton Architectural Press, 2006.

Frampton, Kenneth. "Towards a Critical Regionalism: Six Points for an Architecture of Resistance." In *The Anti-Aesthetic: Essays on Postmodern Culture*, edited by Hal Foster, 16–30. Port Townsend, WA: Bay Press, 1983.

Fretton, Tony. "The Architects Viewed from a Nearby Island." In *Autonomous Architecture in Flanders: The Early Works of Marie-José Van Hee, Christian Kieckens, Marc Dubois, Paul Robbrecht, and Hilde Daem*, edited by Caroline Voet, Katrien Vandermarliere, Sofie De Caigny, and Lara Schrijver, 210. Leuven: Leuven University Press, 2016.

Fretton, Tony. "The Same Thing Said Four Times." In *Articles, Essays, Interviews and Out-Takes*, 6–7. Heijningen: JAP SAM Books, 2018.

Fumagalli, Paolo. "Diario dell'architetto, 26 Novembre 2012: A Flora Ruchat." *Archi: rivista svizzera di architettura, ingegneria e urbanistica / Schweizerische Zeitschrift für Architektur, Ingenieurwesen und Stadtplanung* 6 (2012): 64–66.

Fumagalli, Paolo. *Die Architektur der fünfziger und sechziger Jahre im Tessin zwischen Deutschschweiz und Norditalien*. Edited by Anna Meseure, Martin Tschanz, and Wilfried Wang, 93–97. Vol. 5. Munich: Prestel, 1998.

Fumagalli, Paolo. "Europäische Zivilisation und örtliche Kultur am Beispiel Tessin." *disP—The Planning Review* 2, no. 103 (January 1990): 3–7.

Fumagalli, Paolo. "Il Collettivo in Ticino." *Archi: rivista svizzera di architettura, ingegneria e urbanistica / Schweizerische Zeitschrift für Architektur, Ingenieurwesen und Stadtplanung* 6 (2013): 65–71.

Fumagalli, Paolo. "L'architettura degli anni Settanta nel Ticino." *Kunst+Architektur in der Schweiz / Art+Architecture en Suisse / Arte+Architettura in Svizzera* 46, no. 1 (1995): 28–35.

Fumagalli, Paolo. "Tessiner Architekten: Oder vier Thesen über die Xerox-Technologie / Les architectes tessinois: Ou quatre thèses sur la technologie Xérox / Ticino Architects: Or Four Theses in Xerox Technology." *Werk, Bauen + Wohnen* 73, no. 10 (1986): 2–3.

Fumagalli, Paolo, and Peter Disch. "5 anni di architettura ticinese," pt. 1, *Rivista tecnica della Svizzera Italiana* 63, no. 24 (December 31, 1972): 1222–1253.

Fumagalli, Paolo, and Peter Disch. "5 anni di architettura ticinese," pt. 2, *Rivista tecnica della Svizzera Italiana* 64, no. 2 (January 31, 1973): 36–67.

Fumagalli, Paolo, and Peter Disch. "Questo numero [editorial]." *Rivista tecnica della Svizzera Italiana* 63, no. 2 (January 31, 1972): 38–39.

Fumagalli, Paolo, and Peter Disch. "Questo numero [editorial]." *Rivista tecnica della Svizzera Italiana* 63, no. 24 (December 31, 1972): 1220.

Fumagalli, Paolo, and Flora Ruchat-Roncati. "L'unità e la diversità." *Parametro* 140, no. 7 (October 1985): 8.

Fumagalli, Paolo, Flora Ruchat-Roncati, et al. "Contraddizioni di un territorio in espansione. Due esempi: Valle Maggia e Lugano." *Rivista tecnica della Svizzera Italiana* 64, no. 12 (June 30, 1973): 558–73.

Giamarelos, Stylianos. "Authorial Agents." In *Resisting Postmodern Architecture: Critical Regionalism before Globalisation*, 89–121. London: UCL Press, 2022.

Hanisch, Ruth, and Steven Spier. "'History Is not the Past but Another Mightier Presence': The Founding of the Institute for the History and Theory of Architecture (gta) at the Eidgenössische Technische Hochschule (ETH) Zurich and Its Effects on Swiss Architecture." *The Journal of Architecture* 14, no. 6

(2009): 655–86. https://doi.org/10.1080/13602360903357096.

Hays, K. Michael, ed. *Architecture Theory since 1968*. Cambridge, MA: MIT Press, 1998.

Hays, K. Michael. "Introduction to Jean-Louis Cohen, 'The Italophiles at Work'." In *Architecture Theory since 1968*, edited by K. Michael Hays, 506–521. Cambridge, MA: MIT Press, 1998.

Hays, K. Michael. "Prolegomenon for a Study Linking the Advanced Architecture of the Present to That of the 1970s through Ideologies of Media, the Experience of Cities in Transition, and the Ongoing Effects of Reification." *Perspecta* 32 (2001): 101–107. https://doi.org/10.2307/1567287.

Herzog, Jacques. "La geometria oculta de la naturaleza / The Hidden Geometry of Nature." In *Quaderns d'Arquitectura i Urbanisme: Geografies / Geographies*, edited by Josep Lluís Mateo, 96–109. Vols. 181/182 no. 9. Barcelona: Collegi d'Arquitectes de Catalunya, 1989.

Herzog & de Meuron. "Die verborgene Geometrie der Natur / The Hidden Geometry of Nature." In *Herzog & de Meuron 1978–1988: Das Gesamtwerk / The Complete Works*, edited by Gerhard Mack, 207–211. Vol. 1. Basel: Birkhäuser, 1997.

Huet, Bernard, ed. "La 'tendenza,' ou l'architecture de la raison comme architecture de tendance." *L'architecture d'aujourd'hui* 190 (1977): 47–70.

Institut de Théorie et d'Histoire de l'Architecture, Jacques Lucan, and Bruno Marchand. "Architecture analogue / Analogous Architecture." Translated by Sarah Parsons. In *Matière d'art: Architecture contemporaine en Suisse / A Matter of Art: Contemporary Architecture in Switzerland*, 44–51. Basel: Birkhäuser; Paris: Centre culturel Suisse, 2001.

Kälin, Lina. "Vier Fragen an fünf Architekten." Edited by Wolfhart Draeger and Dieter Bachmann. *Du: Die Zeitschrift für Kunst und Kultur* 546 (August 1986): 68–71.

Kirchengast, Albert. "Der Gotthard als dialektische Landschaft." In *Der Gotthard / Il Gottardo: Landscapes—Myths—Technology*, edited by Marianne Burkhalter and Christian Sumi, 151–61. Zurich: Scheidegger & Spiess, 2016.

Martinelli, Pietro. "Tita Carloni architetto e uomo politico." *Archi: rivista svizzera di architettura, ingegneria e urbanistica / Schweizerische Zeitschrift für Architektur, Ingenieurwesen und Stadtplanung* 6 (2014): 50–53.

Meili, Marcel. "Ein paar Bauten, viele Pläne." In *Architektur in der Deutschen Schweiz, 1980–1990: Ein Katalog und Architekturführer / L'architecture récente en Suisse alémanique / L'architettura recente nella Svizzera Tedesca*, edited by Peter Disch, 22–27. Lugano: ADV, 1991.

Meili, Marcel, Bruno Reichlin, and Fabio Reinhart. "Viele Mythen, ein Maestro: Kommentare zur Zürcher Lehrtätigkeit von Aldo Rossi, Teil II." *Werk, Bauen + Wohnen* 85, nos. 1/2 (1998): 37–44.

Moos, Stanislaus von. "Castello propositivo: Identität, Erinnerung und Monumentalität im Tessin, 1970–2000." In *Nicht Disneyland: Und andere Aufsätze über Modernität und Nostalgie*, 113–28. Zurich: Scheidegger & Spiess, 2004.

Moos, Stanislaus von. "New Directions in Swiss Architecture?" Translated by Christian Casparis. In *New Directions in Swiss Architecture*, edited by Jul Bachman and Stanislaus von Moos, 11–40. New York: Braziller, 1969.

Moravánszky, Ákos. "Formen exaltierter Kälte: Rossis Rationalismus und die Deutschschweizer Architektur." In *Aldo Rossi und die Schweiz: Architektonische Wechselwirkungen*, edited by Ákos Moravánszky and Judith Hopfengärtner, 209–222. Zurich: gta Verlag, 2011.

Moravánszky, Ákos, and Judith Hopfengärtner, eds. *Aldo Rossi und die Schweiz: Architektonische Wechselwirkungen*. Zurich: gta Verlag, 2011.

Otero-Pailos, Jorge. "Surplus Experience: Kenneth Frampton and the Subterfuges of Bourgeois Taste." In *Architecture's Historical Turn: Phenomenology and the Rise of the Postmodern*, 183–250. Minneapolis: University of Minnesota Press, 2010.

Patteeuw, Véronique. "How Exportable is Architecture?" *Flanders Architectural Review* 13 (2018): 245–50.

Peverelli, Diego. "Porträt Luigi Snozzi." Edited by Wolfhart Draeger and Dieter Bachmann. *Du: Die Zeitschrift für Kunst und Kultur* 546 (August 1986): 71.

Peverelli, Diego, and Lucius Burckhardt. "Banca della Svizzera Italiana, Lugano." *Rivista tecnica della Svizzera Italiana* 63, no. 4 (February 29, 1972): 19–29.

Peverelli, Diego, and Lucius Burckhardt, eds. "Banca della Svizzera Italiana, Lugano." *Das Werk: Architektur und Kunst* 59, no. 1 (1972): 9–18.

Prange, Oliver, ed. *Du: Das Kulturmagazin* 906 (May 2021).

Redazione [Paolo Fumagalli and Peter Disch]. "Architettura per la scuola: Le nuove scuole medie," pt. 1, *Rivista tecnica della Svizzera Italiana* 66, no. 10 (October 1975): 26–51.

Redazione [Paolo Fumagalli and Peter Disch]. "Architettura per la scuola: Le nuove scuole medie," pt. 2, *Rivista tecnica della Svizzera Italiana* 66, no. 11 (November 1975): 28–57.

Redazione [Paolo Fumagalli and Peter Disch]. "Architettura per la scuola: Le nuove scuole medie," pt. 3, *Rivista tecnica della Svizzera Italiana* 66, no. 12 (December 1975): 19–46.

Redazione [Paolo Fumagalli and Peter Disch]. "Documenti." *Rivista tecnica della Svizzera Italiana* 66, no. 10 (October 1975): 27.

Reichlin, Bruno. "Figures of Neorealism in Italian Architecture (Part 1)." Translated by Antony Shugaar and Branden W. Joseph. *Grey Room* 6, no. 5 (2001): 78–101.

Reichlin, Bruno. "Figures of Neorealism in Italian Architecture (Part 2)." *Grey Room* 6 (2002): 110–33. https://doi.org/10.1162/152638102317406515.

Reichlin, Bruno. "Quand les architectes modernes construisent en montagne." In *L'invention de l'architecture alpine / Die Erfindung der alpinen Architektur*, edited by Reto Furter, Anne-Lise Head-König, Luigi Lorenzetti, and Jon Mathieu, 173–200. Histoire des Alpes / Storia delle Alpi / Geschichte der Alpen, vol. 16. Zurich: Chronos, 2011.

Reichlin, Bruno. "Un paradigma di architettura territoriale." In *Il bagno di Bellinzona di Aurelio Galfetti, Flora Ruchat-Roncati, Ivo Trümpy*, edited by Nicola Navone and Bruno Reichlin, 9–18. Mendrisio: Mendrisio Academy Press, 2010.

Reichlin, Bruno, and Fabio Reinhart. "Two Houses." In *Tendenzen: Neuere Architektur im Tessin*, Second edition, edited by Martin Steinmann and Thomas Boga, 163. Zurich: ETH Zurich, 1976.

Reichlin, Bruno, and Martin Steinmann. "Zum Problem der innenarchitektonischen Wirklichkeit." *archithese* 19 (1976): 3–11.

Risch, Gaudenz. "Tendenzen: Neuere Architektur im Tessin." *Schweizerische Bauzeitung* 93, no. 50 (1975): 815–16.

Rodighiero, Dario. *The Analogous City: The Map*. Lausanne: Editions Archizoom, 2015.

Rogers, Ernesto Nathan. "Considerazioni sull'architettura moderna: Tesi per il corso di Organismi e storia dell'architettura, 1931." In *Architettura, misura e grandezza dell'uomo: scritti 1930–1969*, edited by Serena Maffioletti, 75–85. Vol. 5. Padua: Poligrafo, 2010.

Rogers, Ernesto Nathan. "Continuità." In *Esperienza dell'architettura*, 130–133. Turin: Einaudi, 1958.

Rogers, Ernesto Nathan. "Éloge de la tendance (tendenza)." Translated by Marie Bels. In *La tendenza: Une avant-garde architecturale italienne, 1950–1980*, edited by Christiana Mazzoni, 90–92. Marseille: Éditions Parenthèses, 2013.

Rogers, Ernesto Nathan. "Elogio della tendenza." In *Esperienza dell'architettura*, 124–126. Turin: Einaudi, 1958.

Rossi, Aldo. *A Scientific Autobiography*. Translated by Lawrence Venuti. Cambridge, MA: MIT Press, 1981.

Rossi, Aldo. "An Analogical Architecture." In *Theorizing a New Agenda for Architecture: An Anthology of Architectural Theory, 1965–1995*, edited by Kate Nesbitt, 345–53. New York: Princeton Architectural Press, 1996.

Rossi, Aldo. *I quaderni azzuri*. Edited by Francesco Dal Co. Milan: Electa; Los Angeles: Getty Foundation, 1999.

Rossi, Aldo. "L'architettura della ragione come architettura di tendenza." In *Illuminismo e architettura del '700 Veneto*, Exhibition catalog: August 31–November 9, 1969, Palazzo del Monte, Castelfranco Veneto. Edited by Manlio Brusatin, 7–15. 1969.

Rossi, Aldo. "La città analoga: Tavola." *Lotus* 13 (December 1976): 5–8.

Rossi, Aldo. *The Architecture of the City*. Translated by Diane Ghirado and Joan Ockman. Cambridge, MA: MIT Press, 1982.

Rossi, Aldo. "Une éducation réaliste." *archithese* 19 (1976): 25–26.

Rossi, Aldo, S. Cantoni, and ETH Zurich Department of Architecture. *Zurigo: Kartenmaterial. Rilievo 1:1000 del piano terreno entro il perimetro delle mura barocche anno 1973*. Zurich: ETH Zurich, 1980.

Rossi, Aldo, Eraldo Consolascio, and Max Bosshard. *La costruzione del territorio: Uno studio sul canton Ticino*. Lugano: Fondazione Ticino Nostro, 1979.

Ruhl, Carsten. "Im Kopf des Architekten: Aldo Rossis La Città analoga." *Zeitschrift für Kunstgeschichte* 69, no. 1 (2006): 67–98.

Ryan, Raymund, and Iain Sinclair, eds. *Gritty Brits: New London Architecture*. Pittsburgh: Carnegie Museum of Art, 2006.

Salm, Karin. "'Ich wollte Architekten zum Nachdenken über ihre Arbeit bringen'." *Schweizer Radio und Fernsehen (SRF)*, June 13, 2016. https://www.srf.ch/kultur/kunst/ich-wollte-architekten-zum-nachdenken-ueber-ihre-arbeit-bringen.

Schön, Donald A. "Design as a Reflective Conversation with the Situation." In *The Reflective Practitioner: How Professionals Think in Action*, 76–104. Abington: Routledge, 2017.

Schrijver, Lara. "Breathing Life into Bricks: The Legacy of the 1970s." In *Autonomous Architecture in Flanders: The Early Works of Marie-José Van Hee, Christian Kieckens, Marc Dubois, Paul Robbrecht, and Hilde Daem*, edited by Caroline Voet, Katrien Vandermarliere, Sofie De Caigny, and Lara Schrijver, 11–21. N.p.: Leuven University Press, 2016.

Scolari, Massimo. "The New Architecture and the Avant-Garde." In *Architecture Theory since 1968*, edited by K. Michael Hays, 124–45. Cambridge, MA: MIT Press, 1998.

Snozzi, Luigi. "Design Motivation." In *Tendenzen: Neuere Architektur im Tessin*, Second edition, edited by Martin Steinmann and Thomas Boga, 164. Zurich: ETH Zurich, 1976.

Somers, Dirk. "Venturi's Discipline." In *Autonomous Architecture in Flanders: The Early Works of Marie-José Van Hee, Christian Kieckens, Marc Dubois, Paul Robbrecht and Hilde Daem*, edited by Caroline Voet, Katrien Vandermarliere, Sofie De Caigny, and Lara Schrijver, 186–193. Leuven: Leuven University Press, 2016.

Stalder, Laurent. "Verwaltete Architektur: Ein Rückblick auf die Jüngere Schweizer Baukunst." *Neue Zürcher Zeitung*, December 12, 2015. https://www.nzz.ch/feuilleton/kunst_architektur/verwaltete-architektur-1.18661562.

Steinmann, Martin. *Forme forte: Écrits / Schriften, 1972–2002*. Basel: Birkhäuser, 2003.

Steinmann, Martin. "La Forme Forte: En deçà des signes." *Faces* 19 (1991): 4–13.

Steinmann, Martin. "La Scuola ticinese all'uscita da scuola." In *Il bagno di Bellinzona di Aurelio Galfetti, Flora Ruchat-Roncati, Ivo Trümpy*, edited by Nicola Navone and Bruno Reichlin, 35–44. Mendrisio: Mendrisio Academy Press, 2010.

Steinmann, Martin. "Neuere Architektur in der Deutschen Schweiz: Ein Katalog und Architekturführer / L'architecture récente en Suisse alémanique / L'architettura recente nella Svizzera Tedesca." In *Architektur in der Deutschen Schweiz, 1980–1990: Ein Katalog und Architekturführer / L'architecture récente en Suisse alémanique / L'architettura recente nella Svizzera Tedesca*, edited by Peter Disch, 10–17. Lugano: ADV, 1991.

Steinmann, Martin. "Reality as History: Notes for a Discussion of Realism in Architecture." *a+u* 69 (September 1976): 31–34.

Steinmann, Martin. "Reality as History: Notes for a Discussion of Realism in Architecture." In *Tendenzen: Neuere Architektur im Tessin*, Second edition, edited by Martin Steinmann and Thomas Boga, 155–57. Zurich: ETH Zurich, 1976.

Steinmann, Martin. "Reality as History: Notes for a Discussion of Realism in Architecture." In *Architecture Theory since 1968*, edited by K. Michael Hays, 246–53. Cambridge, MA: MIT Press, 1998.

Steinmann, Martin, and Thomas Boga, eds. *Tendenzen: Neuere Architektur im Tessin*. Zurich: Organisationsstelle für Ausstellungen der Architekturabteilung an der ETH Zürich, 1975.

Steinmann, Martin, and Thomas Boga, eds. *Tendenzen: Neuere Architektur im Tessin*. Second edition. Zurich: Organisationsstelle für Ausstellungen der Architekturabteilung an der ETH Zürich, 1976.

Steinmann, Martin, and Thomas Boga, eds. *Tendenzen: Neuere Architektur im Tessin / Tendencies: Recent Architecture in Ticino / Tendenze: Architettura recente nel Ticino*. Reprint of the third [1977] edition. Basel: Birkhäuser, 2010.

Steinmann, Martin, and Roger Diener. *Das Haus und die Stadt / The House and the City: Diener & Diener—Städtebauliche Arbeiten / Urban Studies*. Basel: Birkhäuser, 1995.

Steinmann, Martin, and Daniel Kurz. "Experienced Space: Daniel Kurz in Conversation with Martin Steinmann." In *Prix Meret Oppenheim 2016: Adelina von Fürstenberg, Christian Philipp Müller, Martin Steinmann—Schweizer Grand Prix Kunst / Grand Prix suisse d'art / Gran Premio svizzero d'arte / Grond premi svizzer d'art*. Bern: Bundesamt für Kultur, 2016.

Steinmann, Martin, and Jacques Lucan. "Obsessions: Conversation entre Jacques Lucan et Martin Steinmann / Obsessions: Conversation between Jacques Lucan and Martin Steinmann." In *Matière d'art: Architecture contemporaine en Suisse / A Matter of Art: Contemporary Architecture in Switzerland*, edited by Institut de Théorie et d'Histoire de l'Architecture (Jacques Lucan and Bruno Marchand, et al.), 8–25. Basel: Birkhäuser, 2001.

Steinmann, Martin, and Bruno Reichlin. "Critique d'une critique." *L'architecture d'aujourd'hui* 190 (1977): 58–60.

Szacka, Léa-Catherine. *Aldo Rossi, Bruno Reichlin, Fabio Reinhart, Eraldo Consolascio, ETH Zurich, Zurich, Switzerland, 1976*: Princeton University School of Architecture, n.d. https://archive.ph/kNN0w.

Tafuri, Manfredo. *Teorie e storia dell'architettura*. Rome: Laterza, 1968.

Tschanz, Martin. "Tendenzen und Konstruktionen: Von 1968 bis heute." In *Architektur im 20. Jahrhundert*, edited by Anna Meseure, Martin Tschanz, and Wilfried Wang, 45–52. Vol. 5. London: Prestel, 1998.

Venturi, Robert. *Complexity and Contradiction in Architecture*. New York: The Museum of Modern Art, 1966.

Verschaffel, Bart. "Agile Thinking." In *Bovenbouw Architectuur: Living the Exotic Everyday*, edited by Dirk Somers, Maarten Van Den Driessche, and Bart Verschaffel, 10–17. Antwerp: Flanders Architecture Institute, 2019.

Voet, Caroline. "Architecture between Dwelling and Spatial Systematics: The Early Works of the Generation of '74." In *Autonomous Architecture in Flanders: The Early Works of Marie-José Van Hee, Christian Kieckens, Marc Dubois, Paul Robbrecht and Hilde Daem*, edited by Caroline Voet, Katrien Vandermarliere, Sofie De Caigny, and Lara Schrijver, 102–121. Leuven: Leuven University Press, 2016.

Voet, Caroline, Katrien Vandermarliere, Sofie De Caigny, and Lara Schrijver, eds. *Autonomous Architecture in Flanders: The Early Works of Marie-José Van Hee, Christian Kieckens, Marc Dubois, Paul Robbrecht and Hilde Daem*. Leuven: Leuven University Press, 2016.

Voet, Caroline, Katrien Vandermarliere, Sofie De Caigny, and Lara Schrijver, eds. "Prologue." In *Autonomous Architecture in Flanders: The Early Works of Marie-José Van Hee, Christian Kieckens, Marc Dubois, Paul Robbrecht and Hilde Daem*, 6–9. Leuven: Leuven University Press, 2016.

Wagner, Martin. "SCI-Arc, Vico Morcote." *Werk, Bauen + Wohnen* 82, no. 9 (1995): 36–40.

Werner, Frank. "Der nebulöse Begriff der 'Tessiner Schule' oder wie ein Mythos entsteht." In *Neue Tessiner Architektur: Perspektiven einer Utopie*, edited by Frank Werner and Sabine Schneider, 9–85. Stuttgart: Deutsche Verlags-Anstalt, 1989.

Werner, Frank. "Ein Mythos auf dem Prüfstand: Tessiner Architektur, 1980–86." *Bauwelt* 41-42 (1986): 1581–1615.

Werner, Frank. "Lieder, die man nicht erwartet: Neue Architektur im Tessin." *Bauwelt* 39 (1980): 1720–38.

Werner, Frank. *Neuere Architektur im Tessin: Exkursionsbericht*. Winterthur: Technikum Winterthur, 1978.

Werner, Frank, and Sabine Schneider. *Neue Tessiner Architektur: Perspektiven einer Utopie*. Stuttgart: Deutsche Verlags-Anstalt, 1989.

Wiegelmann, Andrea. "Justierungsprozesse." *archithese* 2 (2017): 74–79.

Wrede, Stuart. *Mario Botta*. New York: Museum of Modern Art, 1986.

IMAGE CREDITS

1 gta Archive / ETH Zurich, gta Exhibitions
2 gta Archive / ETH Zurich, gta Exhibitions
3 gta Archive / ETH Zurich, gta Exhibitions
4 gta Archive / ETH Zurich, gta Exhibitions
5 gta Archive / ETH Zurich, gta Exhibitions
6 gta Archive / ETH Zurich, gta Exhibitions
7 gta Archive / ETH Zurich, gta Exhibitions
8 gta Archive / ETH Zurich, gta Exhibitions
9 gta Archive / ETH Zurich, gta Exhibitions
10 Photograph by P. Brioschi. © *Archivio* del Moderno, Fondo Aurelio Galfetti
11 © SIA Ticino
12 gta Archive / ETH Zurich, gta Exhibitions
13 gta Archive / ETH Zurich, gta Exhibitions
14 gta Archive / ETH Zurich, gta Exhibitions
15 © A+U Publishing Co., Ltd
16 © L'Architecture d'aujourd'hui
17 gta Archive / ETH Zurich, gta Exhibitions
18 © *archithese*
19 Mario Botta
20 Mario Botta
22 © Eredi Aldo Rossi, courtesy of Fondazione Aldo Rossi / Fabio Reinhart / *Bruno Reichlin* / Eraldo Conscolascio
23 © Fondazione Ticino Nostro
24 © Fondazione Ticino Nostro
25 © Birkhäuser
26 © Du Kulturmedien
27 © Du Kulturmedien
28 © Thomas Boga
29 © SIA Ticino
30 © SIA Ticino
31 © Diener & Diener, photo: Lily Kehl
32 © Architekturzentrum Wien, Collection, photo: Margherita Spiluttini
33 © Leuven University Press
34 © The Carnegie Museum of Art
35 © Archivio del Moderno, Fondo Aurelio Galfetti
36 © *archithese*
37 © *archithese*
38 © Birkhäuser

ACKNOWLEDGMENTS

This book is the result of a personal curiosity explored in lectures, conference presentations, and papers over a number of years. The earlier forays into the exhibition *Tendenzen: Neuere Architektur im Tessin*, which took place at ETH Zurich in 1975, gradually led to a wider inquiry into the transmission of professional knowledge, examining the role played by theory and criticism in propelling the discourse, as well as the built production, of architecture. These previously published articles and book chapters, written between 2017 and 2021, were significantly regrouped, reformulated, and revised in the present extended essay. The process of critical amalgamation does not allow the tracing of precise correspondences between the book chapters and the earlier versions, although parts of the texts sometimes overlap.

I would like to express my gratitude, first of all, to the conference organizers, scientific committees, session chairs, curators, and editors of the publications listed below, who commissioned the writing in the first place and edited it, often at length: Tom Avermaete, Petra Brouwer, Sofie De Caigny, Ricardo Costa Agarez, Elke Couchez, Rajesh Heynickx, Victoria Jackson Wyatt, Kristina Jõekalda, Andrew Leach, Véronique Patteeuw, Eireen Schreurs, Dirk Somers, Lee Stickells, Léa-Catherine Szacka, André Tavares, Hans Teerds, Maarten Van Den Driessche, and Caroline Voet. Without their interest, encouragement, and additive inputs, this collection of ideas would have never been gathered in the present volume. I am indebted to Moritz Gleich and Jennifer Bartmess of gta Verlag for their trust and patience, and to Hilde Heynen and Paolo Scrivano for opening new perspectives in the understanding of architectural autonomy. Lastly but all the more, my thanks are due to editor Thomas Skelton-Robinson, whose detailed and helpful comments propelled this manuscript away from the original writings and instigated an autonomy of its own.

RELATED PAPERS AND PUBLICATIONS

"The Autonomy of Theory: *Tendenzen – Neuere Architektur im Tessin*, ETH Zurich, 1975." Paper presented at the international conference "Theory's History, 196X–199X: Challenges in the Historiography of Architectural Knowledge," Brussels, February 8, 2017. Published in: *Architecture Thinking across Boundaries: Knowledge Transfers since the 1960s*, edited by Rajesh Heynickx, Ricardo Costa Agarez and Elke Couchez, 2021, 60–80.

"Communities of Practice: Reflections on a Latter-Day Flemish *Tendens*." *Composite Presence: Biennale Architettura 2021*, edited by Sofie De Caigny, Dirk Somers, Maarten Van Den Driessche, Flemish Architecture Institute, 2021, 26–39.

"Constructing the Site: Ticino and Critical Regionalism (1978–1987)." *OASE* 103: *Critical Regionalism Revisited*, edited by Tom Avermaete, Véronique Patteeuw, Hans Teerds, Léa-Catherine Szacka, 2019, 92–104.

"From Tendenza to Tendenzen: Rewriting architecture in the Ticino, 1975-1980." Paper presented at the EAHN International Conference Tallinn 2018, session "European Peripheries in Architectural Historiography," June 14–16, 2018. Published in *The Journal of Architecture* 25 no. 8: *European Peripheries of Architectural Historiography*, edited by Petra Brouwer and Kristina Jõekalda, December 2020: 1115–1140. doi: 10.1080/13602365.2020.1849357.

"'Icons of Compensation': The Swiss Alps as Intercultural Boundary." Paper presented at EAHN-SAHANZ

2019 conference Distance Looks Back, Sydney, 11 July 2019 and published in *Proceedings of the Society of Architectural Historians, Australia and New Zealand* 36: *Distance Looks Back*, edited by Victoria Jackson Wyatt, Andrew Leach and Lee Stickells (Sydney: SAHANZ, 2020), 79–90.

"The Paper Apparatus: Material Traces and Theory in the Exhibition Catalogue Tendenzen, 1975."

Paper presented at the Roosenberg Talks Symposium "Drawings as Objects of Knowledge: Transpositions in Architectural Archives," April 28, 2022.

"The Size of Tendenzen: Between Space, Panel and Page." Paper presented at the colloquium "The Architecture of the Architecture Book" organized by André Tavares at Fondation Gulbenkian Paris, November 2017.

gta edition is a peer-reviewed series of short monographs and edited volumes that take a fresh and provocative look at seemingly well-known aspects of architectural history, thus engaging in contemporary historiography and the production of theory in architecture.

The prepress of this publication was supported by the Swiss National Science Foundation (SNSF).

Series concept
Moritz Gleich, Niki Rhyner, Max Stadler

Graphic concept and design
Reinhard Schmidt, Nadine Wüthrich

Development
Urs Hofer

Project management and proofreading
Jennifer Bartmess

Copyediting
Thomas Skelton-Robinson

Content management
Jennifer Bartmess and Vinzenz Meyner

Printing
TBS, La Buona Stampa SA, Switzerland

Binding
Bubu AG, Switzerland

Typeface
ABC Diatype

Paper
Invercote G FSC 200 g/m²
Munken Print White 1.5 FSC 100 g/m²

This book is dedicated to the witnesses and chroniclers of Ticinese architecture Martin Steinmann (1942–2022) and Paolo Fumagalli (1941–2019).

Cover image
Tendenzen catalog cover (1975). gta Archive / ETH Zurich, gta Exhibitions

2nd printing
© 2025
gta Verlag, ETH Zurich
Institute for the History and Theory of Architecture
Department of Architecture
Stefano-Franscini-Platz 5
8093 Zurich, Switzerland
www.verlag.gta.arch.ethz.ch
verlag@gta.arch.ethz.ch

gta-edition.ch

© Texts: by the authors
© Illustrations: by the image authors and their legal successors; for copyrights, see image credits

Every reasonable attempt has been made by the author and the publisher to identify owners of copyrights. Should any errors or omissions have occurred, please notify us.

Creative Commons CC BY-NC-ND

Responsible person according to EU regulation 2023/988
GVA Gemeinsame Verlagsauslieferung Göttingen GmbH & Co. KG
Postfach 2021
37010 Göttingen, Germany
info@gva-verlage.de
+49 (0)551 38 42 00-0

ISBN (print) 978-3-85676-431-9
ISBN (PDF) 978-3-85676-470-8
ISSN (print) 2813-2505
ISSN (PDF) 2813-2513
https://doi.org/10.54872/gta/4708